A Multicultural Guide to
# Literature-Based
# Whole Language Activities
for Young Children

by
## Dr. Dennis J. Kear
and
## Dr. Jeri A. Carroll

with an introduction by
Tonya Huber

illustrated by Darcy Tom

Cover by Darcy Tom

Copyright © 1993, Good Apple

**Good Apple**
**1204 Buchanan St., Box 299**
**Carthage, IL 62321-0299**

SIMON & SCHUSTER *A Paramount Communications Company*

# Dedication

This book is dedicated to all of us. Our differences in families, habits, traditions, physical appearance, perceptions, language, religion, and arts will never outweigh the similarities we possess as created human beings.

A special word of thanks to the people who used their unique qualities to give input into the selection of books and the types of activities: Diane Kastner, Kim Yasutake, Gertrude Duckett, Gaye Ruschen and Candace Wells.

All three authors are on faculty at Wichita State University, Wichita, Kansas
  Dr. Jeri A. Carroll's area of expertise is early childhood education.
  Dr. Dennis J. Kear's area of expertise is reading education.
  Dr. Tonya Huber's area of expertise is multicultural education.

GA1431

# Table of Contents

## Nonfiction

## Biographies

## Poetry

# Celebrating Cultural Diversity

## Introduction
### by
### Tonya Huber, Ph.D.

*Long, long ago and far, far away. . .*
*A long time ago. . .*
*Before this world existed. . .*
*Once upon a time. . .*
*Many, many years ago. . .*
*It happened like this. . .*
*When the earth was first made. . .*
*In the beginning. . .*
*Once there was. . .*
*In the days of long ago. . .*
*In a time so long ago that nearly all traces of it are lost in the prairie dust. . .*
*and so, good stories begin.*

A Seneca story tells us that very long ago, there were no stories in the world. Because there were no stories, life was not easy for the people. According to the Seneca Nation, Great Stone told the first story to a young boy. Because of respect for Mother Earth, the boy called Great Stone his grandfather. He returned to the Great Stone many times to gather the stories of his people, of the animals, of what things were like when Earth was new. "Grandfather," he would say, "Tell me a story." The boy then retold the stories Grandfather told him to his people. Generation after generation there have been tribal story-tellers. To this day, the Native American oral tradition connects Native American peoples.

Across cultures, across languages, across lands, all peoples share in story-telling—all peoples and languages express the same request: "Tell me a story." Stories help us understand where we have been as a people, what binds us together, how we behave, who we are, and what potentials exist.

# Many Peoples

This selection of stories explores the varied cultures that contribute to who we are as diverse human beings sharing the same Mother Earth. The resources are multicultural and include the diverse peoples who collectively make up the nation of people known as Americans. While the stories of origin and immigration may come from different homelands, the rich traditions and current customs help us understand similar cross-cultural experiences that unite all people.

## Native American Peoples

American Indians, the Native American peoples, are the smallest of the American ethnic minority groups in population, yet represent the greatest diversity. Of some 2000 language groupings in the 1490's, at least 100 (according to some sources as many as 300) native languages are still spoken today. These languages present the stories of more than 400 tribes and nations of American Indian and Alaskan Native peoples.

GA1431

# Peoples of Hispanic Heritage

Hispanic peoples are the largest growing American ethnic minority group. Hispanic subgroups include Mexican Americans, Puerto Ricans, Cubans, Central and South Americans, and other peoples of Spanish heritage. The first European settlers within what we now know as the continental United States were Spanish who established the Spanish-speaking communities that would become Sante Fe, New Mexico, and St. Augustine, Florida, before Columbus landed at Hispaniola, before the English settlements at Sagadahoc and Plymouth Colony established by the Pilgrims.

Mexican Americans are the largest subgroup and historically and culturally bonded to the Native American peoples. Many creation stories remind us that the geographical divisions separating the continent of North America are man-made. As such, they are artificial divisions that separate peoples and lands once intimately connected. These peoples represent the indigenous peoples of North America. Treaties, land cessions, and wars have aided in the division of the land and the people. Though differences and divisions exist, the stories and traditions remind us that all people are related, "mitakuye oyasin" in the Lakota tribal language.

X

GA1431

# Peoples of European Heritage

Americans of European heritage make up the "macroculture," or majority group, in the United States. Varied regions and different countries provide a rich diversity of languages, heroes, and customs from countries as different as Germany, Hungary, Poland, France, Ireland and Russia. As these immigrants claimed regions of the North American continent for their new homelands, the regional distinctions including Midwest, South, Southwest, Northwest, East became known. Colonization and statehood defined new divisions: Pennsylvania, Massachusetts, Georgia, Kansas, Kentucky, Washington, Hawaii–eventually fifty states in all.

"Give me your tired, your poor, Your huddled masses yearning to breathe free, The wretched refuse of your teeming shore. Send these, the homeless, tempest-tost to me. I lift my lamp beside the golden door!"

# Peoples of African Heritage

Just as the story of this country's expansion includes the displacement of the Native American and Mexican peoples from their traditional homelands, so does it include the story of African peoples who were forced from their homelands to this country to serve as slave labor.

Black Americans, often inappropriately grouped together as "African Americans," are peoples initially drawn from a diverse range of cultures and countries in Africa, and later from the Caribbean, Central and South America. Black Americans represent the largest minority group in America. Because of the great diversity in the peoples known as Black Americans, their stories come from all over the world.

GA1431

# Peoples of Asian Heritage

The newest arrivals to the American mosaic are the peoples of Asian and Pacific Islander heritage. While initial immigration to the North American continent from China occurred in 499, major immigration of Chinese and Filipino peoples would not occur until the 1760's and late 1700's, with Japanese and Korean peoples immigrating in the mid to late 1800's. More recently, Vietnamese, Cambodian, Hmong, Laotian and other Asian and Pacific Islander peoples have added to the rich traditions of storytelling in America.

Dad with Grandpa and Grandma in Japan 1956

Mom and me / CHICAGO

GA1431

# Many Stories

While the stories included in this book are intended to be representative of diverse cultures, they are in no way intended to be a comprehensive representation of the multitude of peoples claiming American nationality. Rather, the narratives included in this collection were each chosen as singular, quality works presenting a culturally sensitive story about a person or a group of people. Emphasis has been given to the often unheard voices. Effort has focused on including stories that may not appear in traditional readers, anthologies, and texts.

Because the diverse stories present multiple world views, it is necessary to consider some of the distinctions between cultures in the role and significance of storytelling. The general public in America has a tendency to treat stories as childhood activities, for example, bedtime stories. Yet the current mass media appeal of "children's stories" to the general American public may reveal a more profound need for storytelling–evidenced in the success of such movies as *Edward Scissorhands*, *Hook*, *Fisher King*, *Beauty and the Beast*.

## Oral Traditions of Tribal Cultures

Cultures around the world have used stories to convey tradition and meaning from one generation to the next.

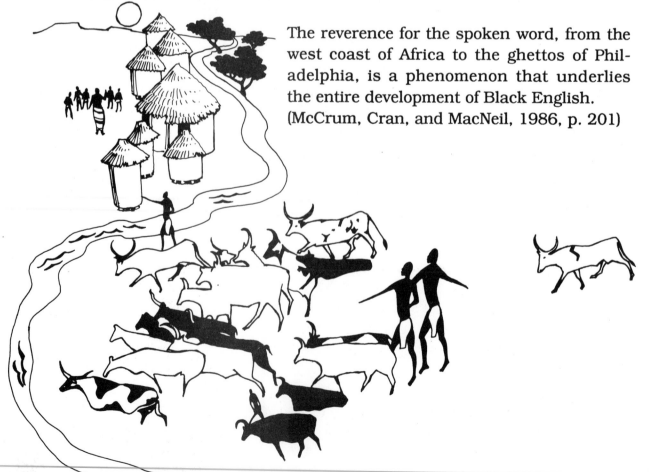

The reverence for the spoken word, from the west coast of Africa to the ghettos of Philadelphia, is a phenomenon that underlies the entire development of Black English. (McCrum, Cran, and MacNeil, 1986, p. 201)

The tribal chief was the traditional "man of words," later to be replaced by the "preacher man." The chief in Africa and the preacher in contemporary America have both provided for their people the voice of wisdom.

Across Native American cultures, a similar reverence for oral tradition has permeated tribal customs. For instance, in the Kiowa tribe, a child may have several "mothers" in the extended family who provide modeling of appropriate behaviors through tribally specific storytelling lessons of the coyote, "Saynday" tales. Coyote tales, "Maa'ii" tales, are also told by the Navajo, as well as by many other Native American peoples.

Since the creation of the world, Native American peoples have tried to live by the natural laws of the universe. Their worldview is "taught" by one generation to the next generation through the oral tradition of storytelling. Native American myths, legends, and songs describe the creation, struggles, tragedies, and achievements of their people.

Ceremonial leaders and traditional healers have learned the stories through attentive and repeated listenings, a significant part of tribal culture that transcends time from birth through life.

The oral tradition of tribal peoples distinguishes their stories from those of other cultures in several ways. A major difference is that stories are not artificially divided into age levels for telling. As stories are told and retold, a rich metaphorical understanding is made possible. Aspects of the story not understood early in life become clearer as the young person matures and broadens understanding through experience and learning. Because of this lifelong retelling of stories, the content of the stories is based on meaning and relationship to tribal history and culture. This places more emphasis on stories in tribal cultures. Myths, explaining the sacred meanings of life, serve as an integral component of life. In the macroculture of European heritage, myths have often been relegated to times past and "storybook tales" for bedtime reading to entertain children. On the contrary, the stories transmit culture and meaning for tribal peoples and, while often used to entertain, have an integrally imbedded learning aspect.

This teaching/learning dimension, particularly true of Native American stories, is another major difference distinguishing stories from different cultures. While many storytellers end with a moral or fable as part of the story, traditionally the story has been allowed to stand on its own in oral tradition cultures. Meanings are gleaned from multiple hearings, from retellings at appropriate times (historically relevant or instructionally related), and through the emphasis placed on knowing the stories.

Traditional tales and legends are told to children, to youth, and to adults as reminders of appropriate attitudes and actions. An illustration is the story told of the non-Native person who challenges a tribal elder about Native American respect for Mother Earth. The story concludes with the following pithy point:

Challenger: Do you mean that if I spit on the earth that you believe she will really feel it?

Elder: Well, even if she doesn't, it would reveal something of your character, wouldn't it?

This brief story would be told following a behavior deemed inappropriate. No moral would be asked for; no lecture delivered. The receiver would be left to think about the story and its meaning. Because stories were repeated, over time and through maturation, ever more meaningful interpretations and understandings were gained. This growth and understanding is lost if stories are divided into age-appropriate categories so that children lose the opportunity to explore the same stories in their youth and subsequently in their more mature years, to reconsider themes, to explore layers of meaning and reinterpret metaphors.

Just as these stories have been told to convey appropriate behavior, so stories have been conveyed from generation to generation by Native peoples about heroes, events, and ceremonies. Attentive listeners have for centuries gathered around the storytellers to hear again and again of special events in the lives of their people; to hear historical happenings retold; to learn of customs and ceremonial ways; to discover in music the stories of their traditions–as such, the stories are for all generations.

Because of the place oral tradition holds in traditional tribal cultures, the word *story* has a much richer and fuller conceptual meaning than it typically has in contemporary culture where it is often associated with children, "fishing" tales, and less significant literature.

One of the purposes of this book is to recognize the centrally significant role of "stories" in many cultures. While a quality handbook on literature distinguishes biography, history, fiction and nonfiction, poetry and song from story, a more holistic understanding of stories imbedded in oral tradition recognizes these labels as names for different types of stories–stories about people, stories about events in people's lives, stories created for illustrative or entertaining tellings, stories intended to document where people have been, stories set in special forms and often told as celebrations through dance and ceremony.

# In the Days of Long Ago

These stories have been collected, annotated, and developed for teacher use in exciting children about reading and learning. But, perhaps more importantly, these stories have been reviewed to awaken in all of us the need for good stories, the need for identifying role models and heroes, the need for understanding where we have been as a people, where we are as a nation, and where we may yet journey as a multiculturally diverse mosaic of peoples.

Boyer (1990) has identified eight stages of ethnic growth, reminding educators that cultural, racial, social, and related factors associated with human development cannot be ignored.

> All socialization emerges from the totality of one's experiences, and those experiences take place in an environment communicating many messages. Such messages are central to the value placed on one's ethnic identity. In other words, one looks for reflections of one's family, race, language, religion, music, recreative practices, and art. Further, such expectations, when not met, deliver a powerful message of rejection, illegitimacy, and questionable academic involvement to the learner. (p. 35)

Boyer goes on to remind educators that

> A psychosocial instructional connectedness occurs within learners when they subconsciously identify with, or relate to, the human profile or human event which constitutes the required content for study in school. This includes the (1) nature of the story, (2) the conclusions drawn from direct storytelling, and (3) the indirect messages delivered as a result of story lines. (p. 35)

Because of the strong connection between ethnic growth and academic achievement, the states of ethnic growth should be considered by teachers from a personal perspective and then from a professional perspective as they select curriculum and instruction. Boyer posits we move from nonexistence in curriculum through states of existence, tolerance, recognition, acceptance, respect, appreciation, and, finally, celebration. (For explanation of these states, see Boyer, 1990, p.1)

Finally, we realize that within each separate culture, certain stories are to be told at certain times. One illustration is that in the Ojibway tribal culture, stories have been told primarily in the winter months when the people needed to be inside because outside work was limited by the severe weather conditions of the northern United States. Seasonal and ceremonial guidelines are attached to many stories in this same way. We hope not to violate those guidelines by gathering these stories together for enjoyment and learning experiences throughout the year. As always, the teacher who is culturally sensitive to her

GA1431

students will need to listen carefully to both the verbal and nonverbal responses of her students as they embark on culturally related readings and activities.

This book is about lifelong learning through storytelling. The stories promote understanding and appreciation of, empathy for, and responsible action toward the diverse peoples born of Mother Earth, particularly those known as Americans.

In Barry Lopez's (1990) National Book-Award novella-length fable, Badger admonishes: "Sometimes a person needs a story more than food to stay alive. That is why we put these stories in each other's memory. This is how people care for themselves."

"Tell me a story . . . ."

## Related Readings

Boyer, J.B. (1990). *Curriculum Materials for Ethnic Diversity.* Lawrence, KS: Center for Black Leadership.

Huber, T., and Pewewardy, C.D. (in press). *Culturally Responsible Pedagogy: Knowledge Base, Application, and Practice.* Bloomington, IN: National Educational Service.

Lopez, B. (1990). *Crow and Weasel.* San Francisco: North Point Press.

McCrum, R., Cran, W., and MacNeil, R. (1986). *The Story of English.* Viking: Elisabeth Sifton Books.

National Education Association. (1987, June). *. . .And Justice for All.* Washington, D.C.: National Education Association Study Group Reports on Ethnic Minority Concerns.

National Institute of Education. (1980). *Students' Knowledge of Textbook Content.* Washington, D.C.: Department of Education.

Quality Education for Minorities Project. (1990). *Education That Works: An Action Plan for the Education of Minorities.* Cambridge, MA: Massachusetts Institute of Technology.

# About This Book

This book represents a collection of activities for teachers to use following the reading of multicultural books to young children between the ages of 4 and 9. We attempted to locate a significant number of books of many different groups of children. We did have some difficulty locating appropriate books for young children in some of the categories and will plan to make recommendations to publishers based on this extensive library search.

The books we found were easily clustered into several categories: homelands, tales, legends, fiction, nonfiction, biographies and poetry. In addition to these children's books, a collection of teacher resources appears at the end of the book.

## Homelands

Books in the Homelands section present information about the lands and lives of the various groups before coming to America to live, or in the case of the Native Americans, living in this country before others arrived.

## Tales

Books in the Tales section represent folk and fairy tales from a wide variety of countries and people. Many have a common theme. Many are similar to other stories we have heard. All are beautifully told and illustrated. Most represent the storytelling traditions of the people they represent.

## Legends

Books in the Legends section again are indicative of the storytelling traditions of the people they represent. The books in this section are mostly Native American, one from South America and one from Africa. We did choose to use the terminology of the authors and publishers in the placement of these books in the category of legends.

## Fiction

Many books in the Fiction section could easily be true stories of real children but are actually fiction. Young children, however, will identify with the lives of the children in the books, whether or not they are of like races or cultures.

## Nonfiction and Biographies

Books in the Nonfiction and Biographies sections represent the real lives of children and adults. The biography of each adult tells about the life of the person as a child, as a member of a family, growing up, making decisions, choosing an occupation and making a difference.

## Poetry

The poetry books offer still one more avenue to explore the beauty of language.

GA1431

# Using the Book

Each book selected is noted with author, date, title of book, and publisher for the ease of obtaining the book from the library or the local bookstore.

Following the bibliographical information is the age group (4-7 or 6-9) that will most benefit from the book and the activities that are presented.

A short annotation tells about the story.

Three or four discussion questions follow. They are of four types.
1. The children are asked to respond with a specific answer from one part of the book.
2. The children are asked to gather information from several parts of the book to formulate their answers.
3. Children take information from the book and combine it with what they know in order to answer.
4. Children are asked to use information from their own experiences to answer questions.

Follow-up activities are provided for teachers to use with their young children. These activities ask children to take the familar things from the book and expand them or to take the strange or new things from the stories and explore them in the safe confines of their classroom.

# Reading to Children

Children need to be read to two to three times daily in a three-hour session of preschool; kindergarten; first, second and third grades. They will learn to love the music of the words and stories as they listen for enjoyment and for information. Read to them in a large group. Read to them in small groups. Read to individual children. Ask parents to come into your classroom and sit in the book area during center time to read to children. Have older children come down and read to the younger children. Read! Read! Read!

Take them to the library as often as you can. Help them learn to choose books about topics of interest to them, not just those put out for them to take. Help them learn to find books for enjoyment and books for information.

Be sure that parents have books at home to read with children. Libraries are a good source. Start a book exchange in your school where children can bring a book from home and exchange it for a different book. Allow children to check out your books to take home as a special treat.

# Homelands

1

# Caribbean

Agard, J. (1989). *The Calypso Alphabet*. New York: Henry Holt and Company. (Ages 4-7).

This alphabet book tells about customs in the Caribbean. It is illustrated in the bright colors of the country. The dictionary at the back provides further definitions of many of the terms.

## Discussion Questions

1. Which word did you like the best?
2. Which pictures were like things that you do at school? At home? At play?
3. What are some of the foods in the book?

## Classroom Activities

### Pan Drums

P is for pan, which represents a steel drum made from an oil barrel. Give the children some pans and let them play their steel drums. Try different "drumsticks"–wooden, steel, leather, cotton. See the different sounds that they make.

Several other books talk about drums. See *Jambo Means Hello*, *Dancing Drum*, *At the Crossroads*, and *Pueblo Storyteller*. See the different types and uses of drums.

### Foods from the Caribbean

Four fairly readily available foods are mentioned in the book: okra, ugli, yam, and curry. Each is easy to prepare.

| | |
|---|---|
| okra: | Chop. Boil with 1 c. (240 ml) tomatoes, a dash of salt, garlic, and sugar. |
| ugli: | Cut open and eat. |
| yam: | Bake. Cut open. Mash and butter or dip into vegetable soup. |
| curry: | Make a cream sauce. Add curry to taste. Parboil apples, celery. Add diced chicken or turkey. Cover with curry sauce. Add coconut, bananas, peanuts, chutney on the top as needed. Serve over rice. |

### Foods or Things to Do from A to Z

Generate a list of as many foods or things that children do at school as the children can think of. Place each beside the right alphabet letter. Illustrate and make into a book.

# Africa

Feelings, M. (1974). *Jambo Means Hello: Swahili Alphabet Book*. New York: Dial. (Ages 4-7).

This book introduces the reader to Swahili words. A word is introduced for each letter of the alphabet. The pronunciation, meaning, and a couple of sentences of description are given. Detailed illustrations expand on the meaning of the Swahili words introduced. An earlier book was *Moja Means One: Swahili Counting Book.*

## Discussion Questions

1. These Swahili words sound different than our words. What words can you remember?
2. If you could find out some other Swahili words, what words would you want to know?
3. Do you know words from other languages? What are they?

## Classroom Activities

**What Starts with A?**

Throughout the year when you introduce the letters of the alphabet, post the Swahili word that begins with the letter and an illustration next to it.

**Drum and Dance** (ngoma)

Get some drums for the children to play and let them dance to the drumbeat.

**Pay for the Products** (lipo)

In the dramatic play center, set up a booth to sell items. Have the children ask for payment (lipo). Play money, beads, and trinkets may be used. Items may be swapped.

**Foods to Try** (embe)

Let the children taste a mango as you show them the "E" page.

**Mom and Dad** (Mama and Baba)

Parents teach the children things they need to know when they are grown. The dads teach sons about building homes and making tools. Moms teach daughters about homemaking. Both male and female children are taught how to care for the young.

Have children draw pictures of their dads on one side of a piece of paper and their mothers on the other side. When they are finished, have them tell you one thing each has taught them to do.

**Conversing in Swahili**

Have the children use Swahili words throughout the day.

jambo (hello)                                    rafiki (friend)

watoto (children)                              shule (school)

Hodi? (May I come in?) Response is karibu (welcome).

# Hawaii

Feeney, S. (1985). *Hawaii Is a Rainbow*. Honolulu: University of Hawaii Press. (Ages 4-7).

This book is a book about colors. Simple, one-word pages state the name of the color and then show photographs of Hawaiian things of that color. At the back of the book is a section About Hawaii which gives factual information about the islands, plants and animals, people and the names of other things that are in the book. The book is quite colorful and shows the brilliance of the islands.

## Discussion Questions

After each of the colors, a consistent set of questions can be asked.
1. What things do you see in the picture that are red?
2. Do we have things like this in our homes?
3. What makes these red things different from the red things we might see?

## Classroom Activities

### Our Town Is a Rainbow

Ask each of the children to make something in his school, home or town that is of each color of the rainbow. Put them into a class book entitled *Our Town Is a Rainbow*. The colors should be in the order of the rainbow: red, orange, yellow, green, blue, purple.

### As Red as a . . .

Give each child a piece of paper and fold it into a number of boxes. At the top write "As red as a . . ." In each of the boxes, have him draw something that is red and label it. He can then read the page to you, to a friend, and take it home to read to his parents.

### Hawaii Is a Rainbow

Leave a copy of the book in the writing center with paper, pencils, crayons. Have the children draw something of each color that is unique to Hawaii. This can be done on separate pieces of paper or on one sheet folded into six boxes.

### Rainbow Pudding

Mix one small bowl of vanilla pudding for each child. Water down some food coloring, one part food coloring to ten parts water. Give the children red, yellow and blue. Put one drop of red on the left-hand side of the bowl. Pull a Popsicle stick through it in a line to mix it into the pudding. Next to the red put yellow. Pull the Popsicle stick through it so that it slightly mixes with the red, but leave some yellow. Drop blue next in the same way you did the yellow. Add red next, and continue to the edge of the bowl. The three colors should make the colors of the rainbow.

GA1431

# United States

Isadora, R. (1983). *City Seen from A to Z*. New York: Greenwillow Books. (Ages 4-7).

This alphabet book presents scenes from the city with one or two words telling about the picture. The illustrations are in black and white and picture people from several races.

**Discussion Questions**

1. What can you remember that begins with *j* (try any letter)?
2. What do you know from our city that begins with *d* (try any letter)?
3. Look at the picture of friends. What things do you think they do together?

## Classroom Activities

**Our City from A to Z**

Ask the children to generate a list of places in your city that they visit on a regular basis. If there are letters that are not represented, talk with the children to see if they can come up with something in the city that begins with that letter.

Assign one child to draw each place. Label the place at the bottom center of each picture.

Place the pictures in a book in alphabetical order for the children to see and read.

**My Own City from A to Z Book**

Place pieces of paper folded into four boxes in a writing center. Put the class book, *Our City from A to Z*, in the center. Children can draw the pictures onto the folded pieces of paper, four per page. When they are all done they should have two extra pieces. One will contain the title page, the other will make a back for their book.

Cut out all of the boxes. Put them in alphabetical order on the floor. Place the Z on the blank piece, the Y on the Z, etc., until the title page is on the top. Staple and take home.

APPLE ORCHARD          BUDDY'S BALLOONS          CHRISTMAS STORE

**Friends in the City**

What do you think the friends in our book do to have fun? What do you do to have fun with friends?

Develop a Fun with Friends chart. Make a list of all the ways children have fun with friends. Place a little illustration next to each. Place where children can read.

# Mexico

Jacobsen, K. (1982). *Mexico* (A New True Book). Chicago: Children's Press. (Ages 6-9).

This easy reader book tells about the geography and history of Mexico. The ways of life of Mexico's people are also covered.

## Discussion Questions

1. Find Mexico on a globe map. What countries are its neighbors?
2. Look at the picture on page 19. Why are husks of corn stored in the branches of trees?
3. A rebozo has several uses. Name some of them.
4. Who was Miguel Hidalgo?

## Classroom Activities

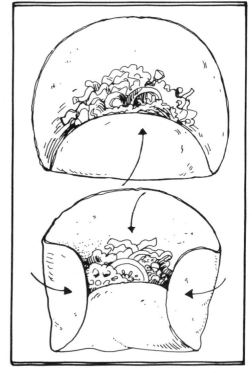

### Mexican Dinner

During a study of Mexico, have your class plan and prepare Mexican food. Set up a food line to include tortillas, refried beans, taco meat, lettuce, tomatoes, avocados, salsa. Give the children paper plates and let them take a little bit of each. When they eat, have them roll the tortilla and eat as bread while they eat the rest with a fork.

### Clothing

Bring in various articles of Mexican clothing and demonstrate their uses. Students could try on the serape and explore the many uses of the rebozo.

If you have enough clothing, have the children each dress up and take a parade to the classrooms near you.

Let each child draw a piece of the clothing that has been brought, using bright colors. Name each piece. Make into a class book.

### Picture Writing

The Maya Indians used picture writing. Tell something you learned from your study of Mexico with only pictures you draw. See if your classmates can tell what you said. Fit the many pictures together into a book for the classroom reading corner.

Individual children may want to make individual books to take home to show their parents what they have learned about Mexico.

GA1431

# Caribbean

Lessac, F. (1987). *My Little Island*. New York: Harper Trophy. (Ages 4-7).

This fiction story tells of a trip two children take home to a Caribbean island. The homes, schools, markets, foods, jobs, and celebrations are shown and explained.

## Discussion Questions

1. What type of things do the children do on the little island that you also do?
2. What things do the children do on the little island that you cannot do where you live? Why can't you do them?
3. Where did the people go to buy food? What did they find there?
4. What types of work did the people on the little island do?

## Classroom Activities

### Homes in the Caribbean

Examine pictures of the homes in the Caribbean. How are they like yours? How are they different? Use construction paper scraps of bright colors to let the children make houses like the ones pictured in the book. Place them on a blue bulletin board which has a large green island in the center. Title it "My Little Island in the Caribbean."

### Steel Drums

Again, we see information about steel drums. Tapes of the music are available. Let the children make drums from "steel" (metal) containers of various sizes. Make sure that you do it when everyone else is outside for recess.

Other books containing information and pictures of drums include *Dancing Drum*, *The Calypso Alphabet*, *The Lion Dancer*, *Pueblo Storyteller*, and *At the Crossroads*.

### Eating the Fish?

There are many types of fish mentioned in the story. Some of them may be available where you live.

Bring in a whole fish for the children to see.

Prepare tuna in many ways for the children to eat–tuna from a can, tuna salad, baked tuna, fried tuna.

### Making Fish

The children see many brightly colored fish when they snorkel. Give the children small pieces of paper and let them make colorful fish with markers. Put them in the sea on the bulletin board suggested in Homes in the Caribbean.

GA1431

# Hong Kong

Levinson, R. (1988). *Our Home Is the Sea*. New York: E.P. Dutton. (Ages 4-7).

This is a story of a boy hurrying through the bustling streets of Hong Kong on his way home from school. He lives on a houseboat in Hong Kong harbor with his family. Tomorrow he will join his father and grandfather on a big boat in their family profession, fishing.

## Discussion Questions

1. Why do you think the boy's mother wants him to be a school teacher?
2. Why does he want to be a fisherman?
3. What is congee and a sampan?

## Classroom Activities

### Sea Pictures

Display pictures of the sea or ocean. Some of the pictures should be of scenes above the water and some should be of scenes below the water. Let some of your students paint a picture of the ocean using watercolors on a white sheet of construction paper. They may want to add a fishing boat on the water. Other students can paint a scene below the water by painting or drawing fish and ocean plants on a sheet of blue construction paper. Display these on a bulletin board or classroom wall.

### City Sounds

Have your class make a list of all the sounds the little boy would hear as he goes through the city from school to his houseboat.

### The Houseboat

Have the children make a house out of a milk carton, covering it with construction paper. Use scraps to make the windows and doors. Oars/Paddles can be made out of Popsicle sticks. Place the milk carton on a Styrofoam meat tray. See if the children can get their houseboats to float.

# Africa

Musgrove, M. (1976). *Ashanti to Zulu: African Traditions*. New York: Dial Books. (Ages 6-9). Caldecott Medal, 1977.

The author provides information about twenty-six different African peoples. Each has a beautiful illustration. With each set of people the author tells about a custom or tradition which in some way reflects African values or philosophies.

1. What was one thing you can remember about this tribe? (Show a picture from one of the pages.)
2. What things can you remember about the clothing of some of these people?
3. What are some of the things that parents do in these tribes that your parents do?

## Classroom Activities

### Alphabet Activities

This book provides an alphabetical listing of twenty-six different tribes. For each of these tribes there is a custom or tradition. Older children could make alphabet books with a separate page for each tribe. The name goes at the bottom of the page. At the top of the page children are to illustrate the custom or tradition.

### Clothful Cloth

The book tells about people in some of the tribes making their own cloth. Children can use natural dyes to make pieces of clothing.

Simmer 2-3 pounds (.9-1.35 kg) of flowers, cranberries, blueberries, or onion skins, in 2 gallons (7.56 l) of water with 2 c. (480 ml) of apple cider vinegar for four to six hours. Use the dye to color pieces of muslin. Wash in cool water. Hang to dry. Children can shape the muslin into pieces of clothing.

To tie-dye the cloth, tie clumps of the cloth with rubber bands before dipping. After the initial bath in one color of dye, children can spoon other colors onto the clumps made by the rubber bands. The patterns that come from the designs can be named by the children.

### Hide the Honey

Materials needed: honey, honeycomb, nut cup, vanilla wafers and crackers. Some of the tribes in Africa eat and sell honey. They find it by following a bird to where the honey is and reward the bird with a piece of honeycomb.

Cut the honeycomb into enough pieces that each child can have one. Hide small cups of honey in the room. When a child finds one, have him come to you and get a piece of honeycomb as a reward. Provide a vanilla wafer to eat with the honey.

# Native American

Ortiz, S. (1977, 1988). *The People Shall Continue*. San Francisco, CA: Children's Book Press. (Ages 6-9).

Ortiz presents a history of the Native American people from creation to the present day. One clear purpose of the book is to instill a sense of responsibility for life. He shows how it was, how it is and how (with hope, luck, and working together) it will be–for all of us.

## Discussion Questions

1. From beginning to end, what is the sequence of events in the history of the Native American people?
2. What types of work did the people do?
3. What types of food did the people eat?
4. How did the people feel at the various times in the book?

## Classroom Activities

### Jobs for the People

Most people have jobs to do, whether their jobs are at work, home, school. Have the children tell you about the jobs of various people. Start with the family.

Fold a sheet of paper into the right number of boxes or lines, representing the number of people in the family. In each box/line name/draw the family member and then list/draw about what jobs he/she has to do.

Expand to people in the schools and then other people they know.

As the children tell about the jobs, ask them to sort them into categories presented in the book: hunters (food gatherers), artists, serving people, caring for people, providing for people, protecting people, teaching the people, leading the people.

Cut the papers to place the jobs in the different categories.

### Working Together

Just how do people work together? Have the children try it out. Give each group of three one piece of paper, one box of crayons and ask them to draw one large (your choice). Watch how they work.

### Before Columbus

For further information about America before Columbus, see *National Geographic*, October, 1991 isssue, "1491: America Before Columbus."

# Navajo

Osinski, A. (1987). *The Navajo*. Chicago: Children's Press. (Ages 6-9).

This book is one in a series of New True Books about Native American people. It provides current and historic pictures of the Navajo, how they got to their present home (Arizona, Utah, and New Mexico), historic information on The Long Walk and life at Fort Sumner, products made by the people and the trading posts where they sell them, housing, religion, education, the Tribal Council, and contemporary life. Several other tribes are included in this series.

## Discussion Questions

When you come to ideas in the book that are common to all children, ask how the ones in the picture are similar to their own and how they are different. (Example: Tell me about these houses. How are they the same as yours? How are they different?) Do this for where they live, stores, housing, religion, education, and contemporary life.

## Classroom Activities

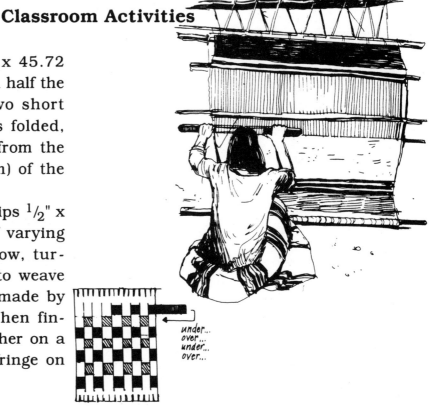

under...
over...
under...
over...

### Weaving Blankets

Fold a 12" x 18" (30.48 x 45.72 cm) sheet of grey paper in half the short way. Fringe the two short sides. While the paper is folded, cut $\frac{1}{2}$" (1.25 cm) strips from the fold to within 1" (2.54 cm) of the edges. Open up the paper.

Give each child several strips $\frac{1}{2}$" x 12" (1.25 x 30.48 cm) of varying shades of earth red, yellow, turquoise, black and white to weave in and out of the strips made by the cuts in the paper. When finished, post them all together on a bulletin board that has fringe on two sides.

### Trading

The stores were set up so that people could trade things rather than pay cash for them as we do today.

In the housekeeping area, set up a trading post on one side and a house on the other. People from the house can make and do things and go to the trading post on the other side to trade for what they do not have.

Older children can trade supplies for the week. One can trade a red crayon for a blue. One could trade two broken crayons for a not-broken one. Make sure that they realize what happens when they trade.

GA1431

# Africa

Williams, K.L. (1991). *When Africa Was Home.* New York: Orchard Books. (Ages 4-7).

This is a story about Peter's life in Africa when he lived there with his family, who were Peace Corps workers. Beautiful illustrations help tell the story of everyday life in an African village. An earlier book *Galimoto* tells about a young boy negotiating with others for materials to make a toy car.

### Discussion Questions

1. What are some of the things that Peter did in Africa that were different from what he would do when he got home?
2. What are some of the things that Peter did in Africa that are the same as we do?
3. If you moved to Africa, what would you have to do differently?

## Classroom Activities

### My Home and Peter's Home

The story tells about many things Peter will have to change when he gets back to America. After you have read the story to the children once, have them tell you about the things Peter does in Africa that he will have to change when he gets home. Ask them how he would do the various things if he were to move to your part of the country. Make illustrations for a bulletin board.

### Cornhusk Dolls

Peter and his friends make dolls and toys from the white stalks in the maize fields. Bring in some cornhusk dolls to show the children what these toys might look like. First and second grade children might try to make them.

### Clay Toys

Peter and his friends also make toys from the river mud. If you are in an area where there is appropriate river mud, try it. If not, have the children make clay toys out of play dough to display in the room.

# Japan

Yashima, M., and Yashima, T. (1954). *Plenty to Watch*. New York: Viking Press. (Ages 4-7).

The authors describe trips from school to home going through the village or along the mountain road and all the things that are seen along the way.

## Discussion Questions

1. What do the children see on the way home from school when they go through the village?
2. What do the children see on the way home from school when they take the mountain road?
3. What do you see on your way home from school?
4. What things tempt you to want to stop?

## Classroom Activities

### From School to Home

Ask the children to take a good look at things on their way home from school. The next day ask them to make separate pictures of each thing that they saw. Under each picture have them write about what they are, or have them dictate to you what they are. Put the children in pairs. Each child puts his pictures on the floor in order from school to home and "reads" to his partner. When both have had a turn, see if they can take each other's pictures, mix them up and put them back in the right order.

Send the pictures home unstapled. Have the children ask their parents to put the pictures in order from school to home.

### Pulling Taffy

Pulling taffy is fun to do, but it is tricky. If you haven't done it before, try it at home first.

To let the children experience what it is like pulling taffy, have them make goop out of two parts Elmer's glue and one part liquid starch.

The children can pull it, snap it, pull it into long strips or snip it and twist it into squares on waxed paper like "real" taffy.

### Japanese Lanterns

See *Moy Moy* for directions on how to make Japanese lanterns.

# Japan

Yashima, T. (1955). *Crow Boy*. New York: Viking Press. (Ages 4-7). A Caldecott Honor Book.

In a village in Japan, a boy from the mountains comes to the school in the village. He does not know and understand the ways of the village children, but he knows well the ways of life on the mountainside. He shares his knowledge of the land, growing produce, and of the birds. Children taunt him when he is young, but when he shows all he knows about the crows, they affectionately name him Crow Boy. His long, daily walks to school for six years are rewarded with an achievement of perfect attendance.

**Discussion Questions**

1. How did Crow Boy get his name?
2. Does anyone call you a different name than your real name? What is it? Why do they call you that?
3. What were some things that Crow Boy knew that the other children did not know about?

## Classroom Activities

**Up Close and Looking**

Using magnifying glasses, examine the texture of different things in the classroom. Have the children draw what the object looks like under the magnifying glass. Others can guess what it is.

Try corduroy, furry coat lining, ribbed socks, cross-stitched pictures, soles of shoes, hair.

**Listening Walk**

Take a quiet walk outside with a strip of adding machine paper, a lapboard, and some crayons or a pencil. Have the children find a soft, safe spot to sit. The task is to listen and draw pictures of things that you hear, beginning at the first of the paper and continuing to the end.

When the children get back to the room, have them get with a partner and circle all the things they have in common. Switch partners; do it again circling things in a different color each time.

**Black and White Writing**

In *Crow Boy* samples of writing and art are shown in black and white. Give the children strips of paper 18" x 6" (45.72 x 15.24 cm), stand the strips the tall way, and have children write on them using black paint and watercolor brushes. They may lay the brush onto the paper, and it will make lines similar to the Japanese ones in the pictures.

GA1431

# Tales

15

# Africa

Aardema, V. (1975). *Why Mosquitoes Buzz in People's Ears.* New York: Dial. (Ages 4-7). Caldecott Medal, 1976.

Mosquito tells Iguana a tall tale that sets off a chain reaction. Jungle disaster is the result, and Mother Owl refuses to hoot and wake up the sun. Eventually the problem is resolved and jungle life returns to normal. Mosquito learns her lesson but adopts a worse habit.

## Discussion Questions

1. What started the chain reaction in this story?
2. What should the mosquito have done instead of hiding under the leaf?
3. How do you react when a mosquito buzzes in your ear?

## Classroom Activities

### The Sounds of Animals

Review with your students the animals in this story and the author's interpretation of the sound each makes as it moves. Ask each student to choose an animal and decide what sound it makes as it moves. Choose one student to make the sound he thinks the animal makes as it moves. The other students then try to guess what animal he has chosen.

### What Happened?

At the end of the story King Lion finally identified the chain of events that took place in this story. "So, it was the mosquito. . . . Mother Owl won't wake the sun so that the day can come." Have your class recite this sequence of events in different ways. For example, all can recite it together. Divide the class in two and have one half recite the odd lines while the other half recites the even lines, etc.

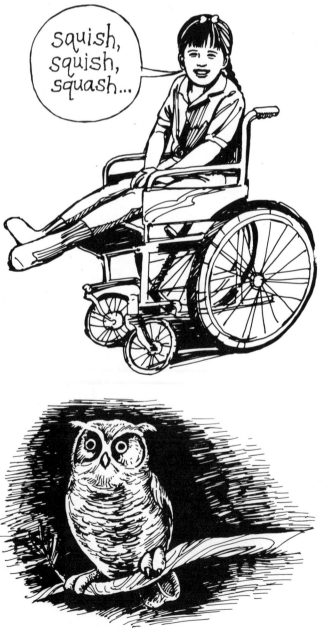

squish, squish, squash...

# Thailand

Ayer, J. (1962). *The Paper-Flower Tree*. New York: Harcourt, Brace & World, Inc. (Ages 4-7).

Miss Moon, a little girl who lives in a rural village, meets an old man traveling on the highway from the city who gives her a paper flower. At his suggestion, she plants it in hopes of growing a paper-flower tree. After a time the old man, called Grandfather, comes to the village with a traveling troupe of performers and Miss Moon tells him that her paper-flower seed has not yet grown into a tree. The next morning Miss Moon awakes to find a paper-flower tree where she had planted the seed.

## Discussion Questions

1. Why do think the old man gave Miss Moon the paper flower?
2. Why do you think he told her to plant the seed that was attached to it?
3. What stories have you been told by adults that aren't real, but most children want to believe them anyway?

# Classroom Activities

### Paper-Flower Tree

Display pictures of many colorful flowers in your classroom. Gather scraps of colorful papers and include different textures, such as construction paper, cellophane, tissue paper, file folders, etc. Also get some tiny beads, pipe cleaners, glue sticks, and tape. After reading this story to your class, lay the materials out on a table or countertop and let your students make paper flowers. With brown construction paper, make a tree trunk and branches and tape or pin it to a wall or bulletin board. Your students can then attach their paper flowers to the branches of the tree and have their own class paper-flower tree.

### Miniature Trees

Ask students to bring a small branch from home. Have them make some small paper flowers and attach them to this branch. Then after the story has been read and retold several times, let them take their small paper-flower trees home to retell the story to their families.

# Mexico

Balet, J. (1969). *The Fence*. New York: A Seymour Lawrence Delacorte Press. (Ages 6-9).

The rich family and the poor family lived next door to each other, but shared nothing. The rich family cooked expensive foods; the poor family enjoyed their smells until the rich father took them to court for stealing the smells of his food. The poor father let the rich father hear the jingle of money to pay for the smells of the food.

## Discussion Questions

1. What do you know about the rich family? About the poor family?
2. Do you think the rich father should have taken the poor family to court? Why or why not?
3. How did the poor family celebrate? How does your family celebrate when something good happens?

## Classroom Activities

### What's That Smell?

Children enjoy determining something by its smell and several smells are familiar to them. If you have a school cafeteria, try to determine the smells that come daily. In dark containers with holes, place aromatic materials such as vanilla extract, chocolate extract, butter, popcorn, coffee, vinegar, etc. Make two of each. Give each child one to smell and have him find his matched smell without talking.

When children have done this several times, place them all in a center with a couple of egg cartons. They identify the smells and place the pairs together.

### The Marketplace

The picture of the marketplace is bright and colorful. Have the children identify things they might see in a market, and draw them on pieces of 9" (22.86 cm) square paper, using bright colors and coloring dark. Post on a bulletin board entitled "The Marketplace."

### The Marketplace, What Will You Buy?

Using the bulletin board above, label each item with a price. Give each child the same amount of fictitious money and have him make a list of things that his money will buy. Look at the variety of things that they have chosen.
Graph the results to show which things were chosen and which were not.

### Celebrate with Rockets

Give each child a piece of black construction paper. Have him construct people out of scraps of bright construction paper and glue them onto the black paper to represent the poor family. In the sky have the child drop drops of bright paint and blow it with a straw to make the bright fireworks.

GA1431

# Portugal

Balet, J. (1965). *Joanjo*. New York: A Seymour Lawrence Delacorte Press. (Ages 4-7).

This Portuguese tale tells about a young boy raised in a fishing village who dreams of going off to other parts of the world to get away from the smell of fish. His dream ends as he is being shot off to the moon. He wakes, realizing that the fishing village is the place to be.

**Discussion Questions**

1. Why is Joanjo called Joanjo?
2. Why do you think he wanted to get away from his home?
3. What happened when he did get away from his home?
4. How long is your name? Do you have a nickname?

## Classroom Activities

**Long Names/Short Names**

Give each child a piece of 1" (2.54 cm) grid paper and have him write his whole name on the paper, one name on each line, one letter per box. Cut out the names and glue them in order on a piece of adding machine tape. Measure each name and record the lengths on a class graph.

On the extra boxes of the grid paper, have the child write the name that he is commonly called. Cut this name out. Glue it onto a second piece of adding machine tape. Measure it. Record these lengths on a class graph. Compare the two graphs.

**Sorting Sardines**

Bring in a can of sardines for the children to examine, smell and taste. After this experience, have each draw several sardines on a piece of paper, color them and cut them out. Place them all in a communal sardine bucket.

Place the sardines in a center with several small baskets. Have the children sort the sardines into the baskets by lengths.

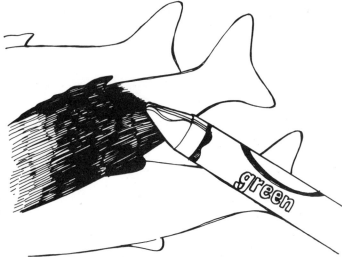

**Fishing Boats by the Sea**

The boats in this story are brightly colored. Give each child a piece of paper or one that has been cut in the shape of the ones in the story. Ask them to examine the boats in the book and then color their boats brightly. Place these on a bulletin board entitled "Fishing Boats by the Sea."

GA1431

# Japan

Bang, M. (1983). *Dawn*. New York: William Morrow & Company. (Ages 6-9).

This story is an adaptation of "The Crane Wife," a Japanese folktale. In this story a shipbuilder finds a Canadian goose with a broken wing in the swamp. He nurses the goose back to health and in a few weeks it flies away. After a time the shipbuilder marries a mysterious woman who makes him promise never to look at her while she weaves sails for his ships.

## Discussion Questions

1. How did the goose turn into a woman? How did the woman turn into a goose?

2. Why did the mysterious woman make her husband promise never to look at her while she wove the sails for the ships?

3. How would you take care of a goose with a broken wing?

## Classroom Activities

### Sail Away!

Collect some pictures and books that show sailing boats. Also provide materials that children can use to construct the boat hull. Thin dial rods can be used for the posts that support the sails. The students can use colorful cloth scraps to fashion sails for the boats.

Some children might like to use their sailboats as props as they retell this story to their classmates.

### Geese, Geese, Geese!

Display several colorful pictures of geese and have students draw pictures of one. Cut out the pictures and use watercolors or markers to color the geese on both sides. These can be taped to string and hung from the ceiling or light fixtures.

### Colorful Boats

Collect scraps of cloth and old clothes. Include plain colors and patterns, as well as different textures. Have students use small pieces of different kinds of cloth to piece together sailboats. Once they have pieced together their boats, let them glue the pieces onto sheets of construction paper.

# France

Berson, H. (1982). *Barrels to the Moon*. New York: Coward, McCann & Geoghegan, Inc. (Ages 4-7).

The French story about trying to unhook the moon tells about a village working together to solve a problem. Each person must do a part. In that way, it is similar to *Stone Soup*, where each person must do a part. In this story, however, the village is not successful. The moon is still hanging in the sky.

## Discussion Questions

1. Why do you think the people wanted to unhook the moon?
2. How far away do you think the moon is? How could you get there?
3. What do you think would be a good plan to unhook the moon?
4. Why didn't their plan work?

## Classroom Activities

### Stacking

Give each child three Styrofoam cups and some glue. Have them stack the cups as high as they can. Compare the stacks to see how high the various stacks were. Ask them to see if they can find a way to make their stack higher. Hopefully after reading the story, the children will find a friend and glue their stack to the other child's stack. If the whole class joins in, the stack could get to be quite large. It will not stand alone unless the bottom one is glued to a base.

### Moon over the City

Give the children squares, rectangles and triangles to arrange a city at the bottom of a large piece of black paper. Glue the pieces onto the paper. At the top make a moon. Cover it with glue and sprinkle glitter onto it to make it shine.

### Jenga

Jenga is a game of wooden blocks that are stacked in a tower. Pieces are taken out, one by one, until the tower collapses. Check your local toy store for the game. It is great fun even for the youngest children.

### *Barrels to the Moon* and *Stone Soup*

Read both of these French stories to the children. Ask them to tell you how the stories are similar and how they are different.

# Hungary

Biro, V. (1972). *The Honest Thief*. New York: Holiday House. (Ages 6-9).

This Hungarian tale is set in the seventeenth century and tells of the times when oppression by the Turks was lifted and the people again had hope. Michael, the honest thief, must steal from the king several times. He is successful and gains the king's treasure, the kingdom, the crown, the state sword and the princess.

## Discussion Questions

1. Why was the king jealous of Michael?
2. How would you have stolen the king's ploughs, ploughmen and teams of oxen?
3. Was Michael right or wrong to steal? Why?
4. What do you think happened to the king when Michael became king?

## Classroom Activities

### The Five Robberies of the Honest Thief

Michael had to perform five robberies. Have groups of children illustrate on large paper the five robberies that were to be performed–not how they were done. One picture would be the six ploughs and ploughmen and teams of oxen, sacks of corn, horses, dinner and a ring. Post these on a bulletin board entitled "The Five Robberies of the Honest Thief."

### Music to Dance By

Michael played various kinds of music–dance music, singing music, sad music, lullabies. Play each kind of music for your children and have them show you with their bodies how the music makes them move/feel.

### Michael's Family

Michael lived with his mom. Have each child illustrate Michael's family structure on one side of the paper and the child's family structure on the other side. Label each. Compare and contrast the family structures.

### Chore Charts

Have the children list the responsibilities that Michael's mother would have and the responsibilities that Michael might have.

GA1431

# Russia

Black, A.D. (1973). *A Woman of the Wood: A Tale from Old Russia*. New York: Holt, Rinehart and Winston. (Ages 6-9).

A wood-carver, a tailor and a teacher go off on a journey. One evening they are stuck in the deep dark forest and have to climb a tree to stay away from the hungry animals. The wood-carver carves a woman out of a tree; the tailor dresses her and the teacher teaches her. They then each want her. They go off to a wise old man to let him tell them which one owned her–the one who made her, the one who dressed her or the one who taught her. The wise old man asks, "Can anyone really ever own anybody else?" The woman is a woman with feelings and chooses the wise old man.

## Discussion Questions

1. How did this woman come about?
2. Who do you think owned her?
3. Why did the three men take the woman to the wise old man?
4. What was good about each of the men?

# Classroom Activities

## Charades

There are five characters in this story. Each does something different. Have the children as a group show you the different things that each character does. Watch as they demonstrate the tasks.

Make ten cards with the name of each character on two of them. Place the name cards in a box. Have a child come up and draw one and act it out for his classmates.

## What Do People Do All Day?

Each of the five characters in the story does something different, has a different "job" in life. Place the name of one of the characters on the top of some chart paper. Ask the children to generate a list of jobs the character does. After they have finished with the characters in the story, have them list people they know in the building, at home, or in their community.

### Tailor

Cuts out material.
Sews material.
Sells clothes.

### Teacher

Reads books.
Teaches people.
Learns new things.

When these are all finished, have children illustrate each person/job and put them into a book of *What Do People Do All Day?*

# France

Brown, M. (1947). *Stone Soup*. New York: Charles Scribner's Sons. (Ages 4-7).

This French folktale tells about how three hungry soldiers trick the villagers into feeding them. Everyone pitches in to make a great pot of soup.

## Discussion Questions

1. What did the villagers do when they saw the soldiers coming?
2. Everyone was hungry. How did they all get something to eat?
3. What kinds of jobs do you know about that are easier when everyone helps?
4. This story comes from France. What are things between France and where we live?

## Classroom Activities

### Bone Soup

Suggest that the children make a pot of soup with everyone pitching in. Make a list of the necessary ingredients and send a note home with each child asking for one ingredient. The suggestion would be that you change the stone to a bone. Children can peel the carrots and potatoes, dice vegetables with table knives.

Recipe amounts are to be determined by the number of people to be fed and the number of children in the room.

| | |
|---|---|
| 3 round smooth bones | beef |
| water | potatoes |
| carrots | barley |
| cabbage | salt and pepper |

Begin boiling the bone in 8 cups (1920 ml) of water first thing in the morning. Brown the beef. Add the ingredients to the soup in the order that they were in the story. Don't put the barley in until ten minutes before all the vegetables are finished.

### Hand in Hand

The villagers learned to share what they had and to work together. This week, have the children work together on whatever chores and responsibilities they have in the room. The helper chart can show the responsibility in the middle with a cutout hand of one child holding the job on one side and the cutout hand of the other child holding the other side.

### Assembly Lines

Some of the activities that you do in the classroom can show shared responsibility. Making snacks is an ideal one.

GA1431

# Vietnam

Clark, A.N. (1979). *In the Land of Small Dragon*. New York: Viking Press. (Ages 6-9).

A Vietnamese version of the Cinderella story. Two stepsisters, one beautiful and one ugly; a father; stepmother; shoes; and a prince. Interspersed throughout the story are "proverbs" related to the story which make it better for older children than for younger.

## Discussion Questions

1. Why did the mother and stepsister not like the beautiful sister?
2. What did the beautiful sister do most of the day?
3. Why did the Prince choose the beautiful sister?
4. Do you know other stories that are similar?

# Classroom Activities

### Cinderella

There is another story in this book related to Cinderella (*Yeh-Shen: A Cinderella Story from China*), and there is the Disney version. Read all three to the children, one after the other. Examine the similarities and the differences. As a beginning look at the family structure of each, the financial status of the family, the work load of the family members, the "finding" of the one to marry the prince.

### Just What Does It Mean?

There are many sayings (proverbs) throughout this story. They include

> Man cannot know the whole world,
> But can know his own small part.

> A man's worth is what he does,
> Not what he says he can do.

Have each child write one of these sayings at the top of a piece of paper and write what meaning it has for him and/or what meaning it had in the story.

### Shoes That Fit

Gather several pairs (or singles) of old shoes that can be kept in the classroom. Trace around each of the shoes and cut out the drawn shoe.

Have the children work in pairs to match the shoes, match the cutout shoes, and then "fit" the cutout shoe to the real shoe.

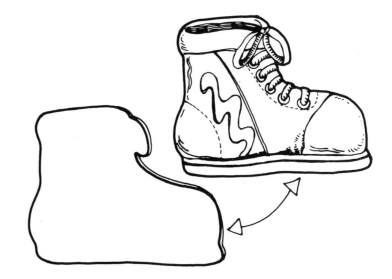

# Wales

Cooper, S. (1983). *The Silver Cow: A Welsh Tale*. New York: Atheneum. (Ages 6-9).

The tale tells the story of how the white water lilies came to be in the lakes of the high hills of Wales.

## Discussion Questions

1. Who was in the family of Huw? What was the responsibility of each one?
2. Where do you think the silver cows came from?
3. Why were the silver cows so important to the family?
4. How do you think the silver cows became white water lilies?

## Classroom Activities

### Cream to Butter

Huw and his family made butter and cheese from the milk of the cow. You can make butter, too. Fill one baby food jar half full of whipping cream for each child. Have him shake the jar and check frequently. After a while it will become butter. Compare the handmade butter with purchased butter–it will be whiter. There is coloring in real butter. Children can put yellow food coloring in their butter or eat it on crackers or bread.

### Milk to Butter

Huw and his family liked the milk of the silver cows better. It was richer. Have the children try making butter with milk, Half and Half, and whipping cream. After they are finished, have them tell you which might have been the "milk" of the silver cows. Which made butter easier? They could assign the different "milks" to the characters in the story and tell you why they would give that certain milk to that specific character.

### How the Flowers Got There

This story tells about how the white water lilies got into the lakes of Wales. Read Tomie de Paola's *The Legend of the Indian Paintbrush* and *The Legend of the Bluebonnet*. Each tells of how flowers got in the fields. Bring in one flower from your area. Have the children examine it carefully and brainstorm things that are the same color and what the flower looks like. Interview each child individually to see if he can come up with a "legend" of how the flower got into your area.

GA1431

# China

Demi. (1990). *The Empty Pot*. New York: Henry Holt and Company. (Ages 4-7).

The Emperor devises a plan to choose his successor. All the children receive a flower seed and a year to grow a beautiful flower. After a year, Ping takes an empty pot to the Emperor and admits that he is the only child in China who failed to grow a flower from the Emperor's seeds. The Emperor rewards Ping's honesty, because he cooked the seeds before he gave them to the children.

## Discussion Questions

1. What do you think about the Emperor's plan for choosing a successor?
2. When have you had to be honest and admit that you couldn't do something?
3. If Ping had not gone to the Emperor's that day, what do you think the Emperor would have done?

## Classroom Activities

### Growing Flowers

Gather as many different flower seeds as possible. Mix up the seeds and give each student one to plant in a pot. You will need to have pots, potting soil and a place to store the pots while you wait for the seeds to grow into a flower. Take time to let the students water and care for the seeds every day.

When the seeds come up, have books that will help each student identify what kind of flower he grew.

### Alphabetizing the Flowers

After all the flowers have been identified, list the names on the chalkboard or chart paper. Let each student write the names on a sheet of paper putting them in alphabetical order. The student may also write the names of the flowers in groupings, such as red flowers, yellow flowers, tall flowers, etc.

### Graph the Flowers

Using the information the children get from the books, have them graph the different groupings of flowers.

### Growth Chart

Give each child a long piece of adding machine tape. Each week, have the children examine their plants, number and draw pictures to tell their growth stories.

# Slavic

De Regniers, B.S. (1976). *Little Sister and the Month Brothers*. New York: Seabury Press.

The little sister lives with her wicked stepmother and mean, lazy stepsister. Sound familiar? The stepmother and stepsister want to get rid of Little Sister. They send her out in the dead of winter to get violets and strawberries. With the help of the Month Brothers, Little Sister can do this. When the stepmother and stepsister get greedy and want more, the stepsister goes to the Month Brothers but only irritates them. They bring their wrath down upon her, the stepmother goes in search and is never seen again, and Little Sister lives happily ever after.

## Discussion Questions

1. Who lived in Little Sister's family? How is the family like yours? How is it different from yours?
2. Why did the stepsister and stepmother get lost forever?
3. What happens in the different months where you live?
4. What were the Month Brothers' names?

## Classroom Activities

### The Month Brothers

Trace around twelve children. Divide your class into twelve groups, one per Month Brother. Assign a month to each group. Have them dress their person like they would have to dress in that month where you live. This will vary depending on where you live. Post these in the room or in the hallway and label each one.

### Products by the Month

In the story the violets are grown in April. The strawberries are grown in June. Contact your local/county extension office to discover which crops/flowers come in which months in your community. Assign a crop/flower to each child to draw. Place these near the Month Brothers that you have posted.

### What Happened to Stepmother and Stepsister?

Ask the children to continue the story. Little Sister can live happily ever after, but use the disappearance of the other two as story starters for the children. Older children can write their own stories. Younger ones can dictate stories to you individually, in small groups, or in the large group.

# Russia

Ginsburg, M. (1974). *Mushroom in the Rain*. New York: Macmillan Publishing Company.

As it begins to rain an ant goes to hide under a mushroom, just squeezing under. As it continues to rain, more and more insects and animals come to get out of the rain. How can they all get under there?

### Discussion Questions
1. Who hid under the mushroom when it began to rain?
2. Why didn't the fox get under the mushroom?
3. Where do you think ants go when it rains? Butterflies? Birds? Mice? Rabbits?

## Classroom Activities

### To Tell a Story
Divide the children into groups of seven. Each group is assigned to make all props for the story. These include a mushroom, an ant, a butterfly, a bird, a mouse, a rabbit, and a fox.

Provide the children with a working box including paper, crayons, glue, scissors, construction paper, toilet paper rolls, tissue paper, fuzzy fabric.

When they are finished making the props, leave them in their groups and retell the story. Let each person "do" his/her part as the story is read. When they have done this a couple of times, have them retell the story in their own group, present it to another group, and then to another class.

### It Grows with Water
Although the mushroom does not really grow like a sponge does with water, you can show the children how something does grow with water.

Provide several sizes of sponges. Cut some into really small pieces. Make sure they are dried out. Provide the children with spray bottles to make rain on the sponges and watch them as they grow.

### Where Do the Animals Go When It Rains?
Have each child choose an animal or insect to write/draw a story about where he goes when it rains. It can be real, or it can be made-up.

The children who draw the story can have you write the words. The children who write the story can illustrate it or make the "hide-out" out of construction materials.

by Jose G.

# Japan

Kimmel, E.A. (1991). *The Greatest of All: A Japanese Folktale*. New York: Holiday House. (Ages 4-7).

A mouse father, in response to his daughter's wish to marry a handsome field mouse, visits the emperor, the sun, a cloud, the wind, and a wall. His search for the greatest of all husbands for his daughter results in an unexpected victor.

### Discussion Questions

1. The mouse ate crumbs off the emperor's table? What do you suppose the mouse ate?
2. Why did the father mouse not want his daughter to marry the field mouse?
3. Why did the father decide that the field mouse was okay after all?

## Classroom Activities

### Which One?

Ask each of the children to draw a male mouse dressed up for a wedding, cut it out and post on a bulletin board. Give each child a piece of paper. Have him make a list of "things" that his mouse has to offer a bride. Post these on the bulletin board next to the mouse.

### Just for a Mouse

Get a small stuffed mouse, just the size of a mouse. Show it to the children.

Provide them with a box of junk that includes empty small boxes for jewelry, small matchboxes, small pieces of wood, material scraps, wallpaper scraps.

Have each child pick out a piece of junk and tell how the mouse might use it for a house or something in a house.

After each child has a piece of junk, have him decorate it as part of a mouse's house or palace and put it up in the room for the children to play with.

### Haiku

The poem at the end of the story is a haiku poem, one that contains seventeen syllables.

Older children may try to write haiku, making sure that their entire poems have only seventeen syllables. Let them copy them on white paper with black watercolors and watercolor brushes. Post on a brightly colored bulletin board, using some of the colors that are in the book.

GA1431

# Germany

Kruss, J. (1970). *The Tailor and the Giant*. New York: Platt & Munk Publishers. (Ages 6-9).

The tailor in the village is sad. He is a good tailor, but he has no business. A giant comes along and asks him to make a coat for him in three days. The tailor agrees to do this, but after one day of work realizes he needs help. He goes to the village, recruits several young women and trains them. Everyone is happy. The giant gets his coat, the tailor gets more business, and the young girls learn a fine trade.

## Discussion Questions

1. Why was the tailor poor at the beginning? Happy at the end?
2. The tailor had a big problem. How did he solve it?
3. What types of chores are easier when many help with them?

## Classroom Activities

### Velvet or Silk?

The tailor makes the jacket of blue velvet and the lining of silk. Provide several swatches of each in different colors, two each of all swatches.

Place the swatches in a box with two hand holes in the end where children cannot see in. Have them feel around to match the velvet with the velvet and the silk with the silk. After they have matched the textures by feel, have them match the swatches by sight.

### Measure It

The tailor measures the giant with a tape measure. Provide rulers, yardsticks and tape measures for the children to measure things. Have each child record what he/she measures and what the measurements are. Let them decide whether they need to use the ruler, yardstick, or tape measure. After they have done five things, have them trade their recording sheets with friends and check the measurements.

### Working Together

Make a large giant's coat from two pieces of butcher paper taped together (about 6' x 6' [1.82 x 1.82 m]). Ask which child would like to color/paint it blue. Hopefully the children will come up with the idea that if they all work together the task will not take as long. Complete the jacket with large gold (paper) buttons.

# Native American

Lattimore, D.N. (1991). *The Flame of Peace: A Tale of the Aztecs*. Harper Trophy. (Ages 6-9).

A young Aztec boy must outwit nine evil lords of the night to obtain the flame of peace from Lord Morning Star and thus prevent the outbreak of war.

## Discussion Questions

1. Why do you think Two Flint was called Two Flint? Why do you think his father was called Five Eagle?
2. How did Two Flint save the day?
3. Does this story remind you of other stories you have read? How?

## Classroom Activities

### Secret Pals

In the story the people give their enemies gifts for twenty days. The children can choose secret pals (not necessarily their enemies) and give them gifts for twenty days (cards they make, pictures, etc.).

### Maize Porridge

The warriors were eating maize porridge. You, too, can eat maize porridge–or at least corn soup or cornmeal mush. The recipe for cornmeal mush is on the back of cornmeal cartons.

### Wash Away the Road

Children enjoy building things and watching them disappear. Provide them with a sand/water table outside. Fill it with dirt/sand and have them build mountains, valleys, etc. Give them a hose which is turned on powerfully enough to wash away what they have built. Build it up again.

### Gingerbread Man

At points in the story, it sounds a bit like the story of the Gingerbread Man who runs away from everyone, one at a time. However, the Gingerbread Man is not successful in the end. Read or tell the children the story and have them tell you about the similarities and differences in the two stories.

### The Study of Science and Geography

There are many different geographic features and scientific events mentioned in the story. As you read about each of these demons, you can talk with the children about why these things might have been considered demons. (river, crossroads, wind, storms, volcanoes, earthquake, smoking mirror)

# China

Louie, A. (1982). *Yeh-Shen: A Cinderella Story from China*. New York: Philomel Books. (Ages 4-7).

The Chinese version of Cinderella dates from the T'ang dynasty (618-907 AD) which is about 1000 years older than the European version. Yeh-Shen is raised by her stepmother and stepsister. She is not allowed to go to the festival. She asks her magic fish bones for a dress to wear. She gets one with golden slippers. She goes to the festival, is recognized by her stepsister, races home, loses one of the slippers, and must return it to the fish bones. Indeed, she ends up marrying the king.

## Discussion Questions

1. Who was in Yeh-Shen's family?
2. How was Yeh-Shen able to go to the festival?
3. Could you think of another way she might have been able to go?
4. If you could have three wishes, what would they be?

## Classroom Activities

### Golden Slippers

Give each child a large piece of paper and ask him to take off his own shoes. Have the children work in pairs to trace around their shoes, laying them on their sides to trace around them. Decorate the shoes with gold and silver glitter or paper. After the children have decorated their shoes, have them cut them out and decorate the other side.

### Whose Shoes?

When the children have finished their shoes for the golden slipper activity, have them pair them up, matching the pairs of shoes. Try to figure out whose shoes they are by the size and shape.

### Her Family, My Family

Have each child fold a large piece of paper in half. On one side have him draw Yeh-Shen's family. On the other half, have him draw his family. Label the members of each family. Find similarities and differences.

GA1431

# Africa

McDermott, G. (1972). *Anansi the Spider: A Tale from the Ashanti.* New York: Holt, Rinehart and Winston. (Ages 6-9).

Anansi is a folk hero to the Ashanti of West Africa, in the country of Ghana. Anansi is an animal with human qualities who triumphs over larger foes because he is a shrewd and cunning trickster.

## Discussion Questions

1. Which son of Anansi was the most important? Why do you think that?
2. If someone were to write a story of how your family works together, what would he say about you?
3. What natural event does this story attempt to explain how that came to be?

## Classroom Activities

### Animals

Help your students see the colors, shapes, and lines that are typical of Ashanti art. Let them use the same kinds of lines, shapes, and colors to paint pictures of their favorite animals.

*Anna's favorite animals*

### Assembly Line Anansi

Look carefully at the picture of Anansi. Have the children tell you what shapes are on the face and the colors. Talk with the children about how the six brothers saved the father.

Gather up the necessary materials. Black construction paper squares, stripes of red and orange construction paper, circles of yellow and triangles of blue, smaller circles of blue.

Place the children in groups of six. There are six steps to making a copy of *Anansi the Spider*. Each child does one part. Number 1 cuts a body shape from the black square of paper. Number 2 places the circles for the eyes. Number 3 places the triangles above the eyes. Number 4 places the stripes on the forehead. Number five places the nose. Number 6 places the mouth. The children do this for six spiders and complete the task by each taking one spider and making eight legs for it.

# Southern United States

McKissack, P.C. (1988). *Mirandy and Brother Wind*. New York: Alfred A. Knopf. (Ages 4-7).

The cakewalk was introduced to America by the slaves in the South. It is said that the one who wins surely dances with Brother Wind. Mirandy goes in search of Brother Wind but ends up dancing with Ezel to win the junior cakewalk. Grandmama Beasley said, "Them chullin' is dancing with the wind!"

## Discussion Questions
1. How did Mirandy think she could win the cakewalk?
2. Where did Mirandy go to look for Brother Wind?
3. Where else might she have gone to catch him?
4. Why did people who watched the winners think that they had been dancing with the wind?

## Classroom Activities

### Where Is the Wind?
On a slightly windy day, take the children out for a walk in the area. Every once in a while stop and stand still to feel the wind. Try to see if there is any one place where it is windier than others and determine why that might be.

For other windy activities, see the activities listed for *Gilberto and the Wind*.

### Cakewalk
The cakewalk that is done today in many schools for Fun Night is one where people march around a circle on numbered squares until the music stops. When the music stops, a number is drawn from a can and that person wins the cake.

To use this with the children, bring in cupcakes, one for each child. Place squares on the floor with matching squares in a can. Use information from what you are studying (colors, beginning consonant sounds, contractions, compound words, spelling words, etc.)

Place each child on a square to begin. Play music. When the music stops, call out one piece of information from the can. The child who matches picks up the square that he is standing on, brings it to you and exchanges it for a cupcake. Continue until each child has a cupcake.

### Scarves in the Wind
Bring in old scarves. Tie them to the children's wrists. Let them wear them outside on a windy day or run in the gym with them on.

# India

Quigley, L. (1959). *The Blind Men and the Elephant*. New York: Charles Scribner's Sons. (Ages 6-9).

The story tells about how the six blind men each described only one part of an elephant and argued over what it did look/feel like. The moral was that to find out the truth, one must put all the parts together.

## Discussion Questions

1. How did the blind men get from one place to another?
2. Why did they get into an argument about what an elephant looked like?
3. Can you think of things that would seem funny if you only knew about parts of them?

## Classroom Activities

### Six in Line

Ask the children to get into groups of six and put themselves in order from smallest to tallest. When they think they have done this correctly, have them get another group to check to see if they are right.

Take a tour of the building, walking one behind the other in a line–using their eyes. They can talk about how hard it was to stay together, even with their eyes open.

### What's in the Bag?

Place a large object in a paper bag. Ask six different children to come forward and feel only one part of the object. You will have to guide their hands to the one part. Ask them to describe what they touched.

When all have touched at least one part, have each tell about his part. See if they can put the parts together verbally to figure out what it was that they touched.

### Pin the Trunk on the Elephant

Trace a large front view of an elephant's face. Stuff one leg of a pair of grey panty hose with paper to make a trunk. Blindfold each child and have him try to put the trunk on the elephant. Young children do not like to be blindfolded. Try a large grocery sack over the head. You can see out of the bottom but not to put the trunk on the elephant.

# Japan

Say, A. (1991). *Tree of Cranes*. Boston: Houghton Mifflin Company. (Ages 4-7).

The story tells about how a Japanese boy celebrates his first Christmas in Japan.

## Discussion Questions

1. What different things did the boy see his mother doing that were unusual?
2. How was his Christmas tree different from yours? How was it the same as yours?
3. Why couldn't the little boy play with the present that he got on Christmas?
4. What could he have done that day if there was no snow?

## Classroom Activities

### Paper Cranes

Young children will find it difficult to learn to fold the paper cranes. By second grade they could try it. However, it should be done in small groups of three to five where each child can be closely monitored by the adult.

As a substitute for younger children, have them make a two-part bird. One part is the body of the bird. Make a slit in the body. Place a set of wings through it. Hang it on the tree.

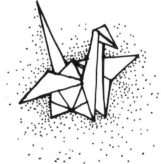

### Christmas Trees at Home

Homemade pinecone ornament

Look carefully at the Christmas tree in the book which is decorated with paper cranes and candles.

Let the children tell you about how they decorate their own Christmas trees at home, including any special ornaments or decorations that are special to them.

### Paper Christmas Tree Decorations

Get an artificial tree for your classroom. Place the miniature lights on it. Let the children make paper decorations for it. Start with the above paper cranes.

Trace around cookie cutters on construction paper. Decorate with glitter.

Make paper chains from 1" x 6" (2.54 x 15.24 cm) strips of paper. Put child's name on each strip.

Make circles from 1" x 6" (2.54 x 15.24 cm) strips. Put one inside the other. Fill with tissue paper.

Cut out the decorations from old Christmas cards. Mount on gold paper. Hang.

Glue child's picture onto a Christmas tree piece of paper, decorated with sequins.

GA1431

# Africa

Steptoe, J. (1987). *Mufaro's Beautiful Daughters*. New York: Lothrop, Lee & Shepard Books. (Ages 4-7).

The king must choose a wife, and he is choosing from between the two daughters of Mufaro, one bad tempered and one kind and sweet. In order to do so, the king changes himself into a hungry boy, an old woman and a snake to see what the personalities of the two daughters are. Guess who he chooses!

## Discussion Questions

1. Was Manyara kind to the people in the forest? What did she do that was unkind?
2. Was Nyasha kind to the people in the forest? What happened?
3. Do you know any stories that are similar to this? What are they? What happened in the stories?
4. Why did Manyara become a servant? Why did Nyasha become the queen?

## Classroom Activities

### Sing to the Plants

Does singing do anything to help the plants grow? Bring in two plants. Treat them the same, but ask the children to sing to the one each day, taking the other into the hall so it cannot hear. Examine the plants weekly to see if there is any difference.

### Bands for the Hair

In the story the women wear bands of various kinds around their heads. Have the children make bands. Use cloth, gold or silver braid, or construction paper. Tie on the bands and wear them throughout the day.

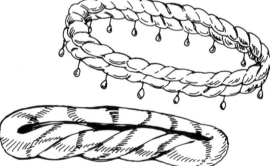

### The Balancing Act

Many of the stories in this book talk about and show pictures of people balancing things on their heads. Let your children try. A block from the block area would make something to hold on the head a bit slippery but unbreakable. After they have practiced a while, have a balancing act. Let the children show you what they can do while they are still balancing things on their heads.

### Beauty and the Beast

Read *Beauty and the Beast*, *A Woman of the Wood*, or *The Frog Prince*. Let the children make comparisons between the stories.

# Japan

Tejima. (1990). *Ho-Limlim: A Rabbit Tale from Japan*. New York: Philomel Books. (Ages 4-7).

*Ho-Limlim* is based on a tale from the oral tradition of the Ainu people, a primitive and disappearing race of the Hokkaido province. After one last adventure far from his home, an aging rabbit decides he prefers to rest in his own garden and let his children and grandchildren bring him good things to eat.

## Discussion Questions

1. What caused the rabbit to mistake seaweed for a whale, logs for people fighting, and clouds for smoke?
2. What does the phrase "ho-limlim, ho-limlim" represent?
3. Make up a word that would represent the sound you make when you run through tall grass.

## Classroom Activities

### Rabbits

On a sheet of construction paper have your students draw one of the scenes from the story leaving out the rabbit. The rabbit can be included into the picture by gluing cotton balls onto the picture in the shape of a rabbit.

Scraps of construction paper can be used for ears, feet, etc. Glue on googly eyes.

### Young and Old Alike

Give each student a sheet of paper and have him fold it into thirds. Open the paper and label the first column "Young," the second column "Both," and the third column "Old." In the first column (Young), he should make a list of those things he likes and can do, but his parents don't like or can't do. In the second column (Both), he should make a list of those things both he and his parents like and can do. In the third column (Old), he should make a list of those things his parents and other older people like and can do, but he doesn't like or can't do.

### A Visit to the Elderly

Make some cookies in the classroom that the children can take to a nearby nursing home. Take sugar cookies to be sure the people can chew them.

GA1431

# Laos (Hmong)

Xiong, Blia, and Spagnoli, C. (1989). *Nine-in-One, Grr! Grr!* San Francisco, CA: Children's Book Press.

This Hmong tale, told to a storyteller by Blia Xiong, was first heard by her when she was a young child in Laos and carried with her as she immigrated to the United States after the war. It tells the story of why tigers have not overrun the world today, eating everything in sight.

## Discussion Questions

1. Why did the tiger go off to find the great Shao?
2. What happened when the tiger tried to remember Shao's words?
3. Why was the bird so concerned about the tiger having nine cubs a year?
4. What would happen in your city if it had tigers running loose in the streets?

## Classroom Activities

### The Story Cloth

The illustrations in this story are shown in the tradition of embroidered story cloths. A pattern surrounds each picture which is entirely colored in.

Ask each child to choose his favorite part of the story and illustrate using colors and watercolor paper. When he has colored his picture, make a watercolor wash to fill in the empty space. Mount the picture on a piece of paper, larger than the picture itself, to form a 1" (2.54 cm) border all the way around.

In the 1" (2.54 cm) border, devise a pattern similar to the patterns presented in the book. If you put the pictures in sequence, you can post them in the hall in sequential order to retell the story.

### Wild Animals/Tame Animals

The tiger in the story is a wild animal, living in the wild. Children now see these wild animals mostly in zoos or reserves. Some animals, however, are tame and live among people.

Have the children generate a list of animals, all the ones that they can think of. Assign each child to illustrate at least one. As a group sort them into wild and tame animals. The children may suggest other groupings (farm, zoo, pets, etc.).

GA1431

# China

Young, E. (1989). *Lon Po Po: A Red-Riding Hood Story from China*. New York: Scholastic, Inc. (Ages 4-7). Caldecott Medal, 1990.

The three daughters of a Chinese country woman were left at home alone while their mother went off to see their grandmother. A clever wolf saw her leave and decided to eat the daughters. He got into the house, but the eldest daughter realized that he was a wolf and tricked him into letting the sisters climb the gingko tree to get some gingkos for him, to give him eternal life. They climbed up and again tricked the wolf into crawling into a basket which they raised and dropped him from. The third time did the trick.

## Discussion Questions

1. How did the children feel when their mother left them alone?
2. Why did the mother have to visit the grandmother? What do you suppose she took with her?
3. How did the three girls work together to solve their problem?

## Classroom Activities

### Little Red Riding Hood

After you have read the story *Lon Po Po*, ask the children if they know a story that is similar. Read *Little Red Riding Hood* to the children. Graph the differences/similarities.

   Went to see grandmother
   Reason to see grandmother
   Tricked the wolf
   How the wolf was tricked
   How the wolf died
   What the girl(s) told their mother

### Wolf Parts

Show the children a picture of a wolf from one of the stories or from an encyclopedia. Have them list the various parts of a wolf–eyes, nose, mouth, teeth, ears, tail, legs, paws, etc.

Use the language pattern from one of the stories–"My, what big eyes you have," or "Po Po, your foot has bush on it"–for each of the wolf parts. Let the children tell you the wolf's excuse for having wolf parts instead of grandmother parts.

Role-play either story and embellish it with the children's made-up parts.

GA1431

# Legends

GA1431

# Cherokee

Cohlene, T. (1990). *Dancing Drum: A Cherokee Legend*. Mahwah, NJ: Watermill Press. (Ages 6-9).

The Cherokee people were first disturbed by the scorching sun which did not allow their plants to grow. In an attempt to get the sun to obey, it became angry and would not shine, bringing cold to the country and then as the sun became sad, rain. A young boy, Dancing Drum, plays his drum for the sun and Grandmother Sun once again would shine on the people. Factual information about the Cherokee people appears at the end of the book.

## Discussion Questions

1. How did the people try to get the sun to stop shining?
2. Why was the sun so important?
3. What types of things do you have at home that require sun? At school?
4. What did Dancing Drum do to please the sun, and what happened when he did?

# Classroom Activities

### Cherokee Village

Information about how the Cherokee villages were set up is in the information at the back of the book. In the center of the village was a large, round Council House. The people lived in domed houses and the entire village was surrounded by a palisade—three rows of upright poles. Let children make a model Cherokee village.

### Domed Houses

Give each child the bottom half of a Styrofoam cup for the house.
The top will be a cone-shaped cup covered with dried grass.

### Palisade

The palisade will be made of Popsicle sticks glued to a circular piece of rope.

### The Council House

Use a piece of paper 18" (45.72 cm) in length, 4" (10.16 cm) high, shaped into a circle. The cone-shaped roof will be made from a large piece of butcher paper, again covered with dry grass.

# Comanche

De Paola, T. (1983). *The Legend of the Bluebonnet*. New York: G.P. Putnam's Sons. (Ages 4-7).

This tale is about the origin of the Bluebonnet (Lupine, Buffalo Clover, Wolf Flower, El Conejo) and the courage of a young girl as she throws her doll into the fire to save her people.

## Discussion Questions

1. Why was the little girl called She-Who-Is-Alone?
2. Who do you suppose took care of her?
3. Why was rain so important to the Comanche people?
4. How did the people finally get the rains to come?

## Classroom Activities

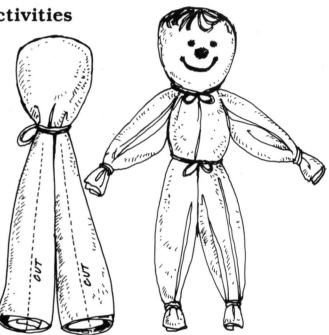

### Cloth Dolls

She-Who-Is-Alone had a doll made of buckskin. Each child can make a cloth doll from a dish towel or a diaper.

Roll the cloth the long way. Fold it in half. Tie a piece of string around the top to make a head. Divide the rest of the cloth in half. Cut it up the middle. Divide each half in half and cut it up the middle. Tie off each quarter to make arms and legs.

Let the child paint a face on the doll—eyes, nose, and mouth—with paint using a Q-tip.

### Plants Need Rain

In the story the people were hungry because there was no rain to grow the food. In order to show the children that plants need water to grow, plant seeds. When they are healthy, stop watering one and watch to see what happens.

### Food Bank

Hunger is not an unusual thing, even today with the children we see. The Comanche were hungry because there was no rain to grow food. Our children may be hungry for other reasons. Discuss the reasons why people today might be hungry.

In one corner, make a bank safe out of an old box. Ask each child to bring a can of food whenever he thinks about it to put in the class food bank. When the bank is full, call your local food bank and ask them to pick it up and thank the children.

# Native American

De Paola, T. (1988). *The Legend of the Indian Paintbrush.* New York: G.P. Putnam's Sons. (Ages 4-7).

De Paola recounts a story of how the Indian paintbrush, a wildflower found in Wyoming, Texas, and the high plains, came to be. The inspiration for the story came from a copy of *Texas Wildflowers, Stories and Legends.*

## Discussion Questions
1. Why did Little Gopher feel that he was different from the other children?
2. What could he do that others could not?
3. He painted on the skins of animals. What things do we paint on?
4. What are things you cannot do that older children can do?
5. What are things you can do and like to do that make you different from others?

# Classroom Activities

## Stone Painting

Little Gopher made paints from stones and used stones to paint on. Children will enjoy finding just the right rock to paint. To begin with, let them color the rock with blueberries or cranberries. (Use aprons to protect the clothing.) Several smaller stones can be used and then glued together to make a sculpture.

## Nature Paintings

Little Gopher painted with the Indian paintbrush, a wildflower that he found. Children, too, can paint with things from nature.

Give each child a white piece of paper and suggest that he draws something that is found in nature. Take the children outside and let them "paint" with the things in nature. Try mud, leaves, flowers. Just rubbing them hard onto the paper will make a nice color.

LEAVES CREATED BY RUBBING GREEN LEAVES AND WEEDS

YELLOW DANDELION RUBBED TO CREATE THE SUN

DIRT AND CLAY RUBBED AND SMEARED TO CREATE GROUND

LINES MADE WITH A STICK THAT IS PRESSED INTO BERRIES

## Flower Dyes

To paint objects, use some dyes made from flowers. Gather about two dozen flowers. Cover the flowers with water and simmer for a couple of hours. Add 1 cup (240 ml) apple cider vinegar to help set the dye.

To make a bookmark, use pinking shears to cut a piece of muslin in the shape of a bookmark. Let the children use Q-tips to "paint" onto the muslin.

GA1431

# South America

Duarte, M. (1968). *The Legend of the Palm Tree*. New York: Grosset & Dunlap Publishers. (Ages 4-7).

This story was translated as a gesture of goodwill between the children of North and South America. It tells of how the palm tree saved the Indians of Brazil from the scorching sun, drought, and death. The uses of the various parts of the palm tree are explained.

## Discussion Questions

1. Why did the boy and his family move? Where were they going?
2. How did the palm tree save the people?
3. What do you know about the trees in the place where you live? What do you use them for?

## Classroom Activities

### Coconut

Have the children examine the outside of a coconut. Give each group of six children one coconut with the chore to crack it. Send them outside and let them try. If they get it open, have them examine the insides, taste the "milk" (not too much), and the coconut.

Bring in coconut products and compare them to the coconut.

### Palm Branches

Near Palm Sunday the florists will have palm branches. Bring in some for your children to see, making sure that there are enough that each child can have one. Compare the "leaves" with the leaves of the trees in your area.

Staple five or six "leaves" close together onto a strip of paper. Show the children how to weave. You can get a square "coaster" by weaving six "leaves" into the six stapled ones. Cut off the remains.

### Sharing the Harvest

The young Indian in the story took the coconuts to other Indians. Visit an orchard in your area, collect some of the fruits, and take them to the nursing home or to a food kitchen in your area to share with others.

GA1431

# Native American

Friskey, M. (1959). *Indian Two Feet and His Horse.* New York: Scholastic Book Services. (Ages 4-7).

## Discussion Questions

1. What were some of the things that Indian Two Feet could do?
2. Why do you think Indian Two Feet was called Indian Two Feet?
3. If you wanted to go places to do things, what would you wish for?
4. Why do you think the horse liked Indian Two Feet?

# Classroom Activities

## Way to Go

There are many ways to go places. Give each child a piece of paper and ask him to draw a picture of somewhere he can go and how he can get there. Based upon the experiences of your children, the modes of transportation will differ. Encourage different types of transportation from each child. Some might include bike, trike, roller skates, skateboard, scooter, wagon, bus, train, plane, school bus, car, van, mini van, truck, station wagon, walk alone, walk with someone, run, skip.

Use a simple sentence at the bottom of each, using the same language pattern throughout to make a class book. Try "I can get to _____ in/on my _____."

## Can Do–Can't Do

Indian Two Feet could do many things but there were some things he could not do. Let each child draw a picture of something he can do and something he cannot do. Put them on a bulletin board where one side is entitled "Can Do" and the other entitled "Can't Do."

| CAN DO | CAN'T DO |
|---|---|
|  |  |

## Care for the Animals

Indian Two Feet had to care for his horse. Ask the children what he did to take care of the horse.

Plan to get a class pet for the room–obviously not a horse. Make a list of things that must be done to care for the pet. Assign different children the responsibility throughout the year.

GA143

# Native American

Goble, P. (1985). *The Great Race of the Birds and Animals.* New York: Bradbury Press. (Ages 6-9).

Goble presents the myths of the Cheyenne and Sioux in this story of how the people came to power over the animals and were also charged with the care of Creation.

### Discussion Questions
1. Why was The Great Race run?
2. Who did you think would win?
3. How did the Magpie win?
4. How is the Magpie like people?

## Classroom Activities

### Sort the Animals
Look for pictures of animals, some with two legs and some with four legs. Have the children cut them out and mount them on index cards. Place the cards in a center and have them group them as they will. At some point, have them group them into ones with two legs and ones with four legs.

### All the Animals from Near and Far
Give each child a piece of paper to fold into four boxes. Ask each child to draw four animals, one in each box. When he is finished, have him cut the animals out. Put them all on a bulletin board, sorting them into two-legged and four-legged animals.

### Buffalo with Hairy Chin
Let each child trace around a pattern of a buffalo onto a sheet of brown paper. Cover the buffalo with glue and pat into a flat pan of coffee grounds. To make hair for the chin, glue on brown yarn.

### Feather Collecting
Gather different kinds of feathers for the children to examine. The zoo or a hunter may save some for you. Be sure to spray them for lice before bringing them into the room. Sort the feathers into piles by kinds or colors. Examine them closely to see the various colors in each feather.

GA1431

# Africa

Grifalconi, A. (1986). *The Village of Round and Square Houses*. Boston: Little, Brown and Company. (Ages 4-7).

This book tells the story of how the men came to live in square houses and women came to live in round houses in the village of Teos.

## Discussion Questions

1. Why did the men and women of this village live in different places?
2. What do you think caused the people to turn gray?
3. What problems do you think might arise if the men lived in one place and the women in another?

## Classroom Activities

### Reading the Story

Place the oldest children in a row of chairs, and have the younger children sit in front of them. In the story the oldest person sits higher on a stool.

### Sorting: Round Houses (girls) and Square Houses (boys)

Provide a table with round objects, square objects and little dolls of boys and girls. Cut out two large shapes, one circular and one square. Have children sort objects.

### What Have You Learned Today?

In the story the grandfather asked the children one by one what they had learned today. At the end of the day, call each child up to sit on your "boney knee" and ask him what he learned today.

### Yummy Yams

Both *Ashanti to Zulu* and this book talk about white yams. Get yams at the produce department (they will probably not be white). Examine, cut, cook and eat them. Butter would be good on them. Brown sugar could be added.

### Bowls and Towels

Have the younger children carry in bowls of warm water and towels to wash hands before and after eating. (Change the water frequently.)

### Stew

In this story and in the *Ashanti to Zulu* book, people are described as eating the stew from a common bowl with sticks of fou-fou. Although we cannot make the fou-fou or eat from common bowls, children can eat individual portions of stew with crackers or strips of toast. As children get ready to eat, the oldest dips first into his individual bowl, and then the others dip in order of age, the youngest starting to eat last.

# Fiction

GA1431

# Arab

Alexander, S. (1983). *Nadia the Willful*. New York: Pantheon Books. (Ages 6-9).

When her favorite brother disappears in the Arab desert forever, Nadia refuses to let him be forgotten, even though her father issues a bitter decree that his name shall not be uttered.

## Discussion Questions

1. What is a sheik?
2. Why do you think Tarik, Hamed's father, decreed that no one ever speak of Hamed again?
3. Why did Nadia's father call her wise?

## Classroom Activities

### Sand Pictures

Have your students make three-dimensional pictures of a desert scene. On a sheet of construction paper draw the outline of some sand hills. Cover this area with glue and pat the construction paper in a tray filled with sand. On another sheet of construction paper draw, color, and cut out a camel with a rider, trees for an oasis, a sun, and some clouds. Arrange and glue these on the sand hill picture.

### Memory

Read or tell a short story to your students and ask them to retell the story to you. Record the retelling on tape. Then read or tell another short story to your class. With this second story get your students involved in the story. Have them do some actions as part of the story. Ask them questions about the story as you tell it. Include some actions as you read/tell the story. Show pictures that describe some of the scenes or characters. Now ask your students to retell the story and record this retelling on tape. Have your class compare the two retellings. Which story were they better able to retell? Which retelling included more details? Which retelling was a closer match to the original story?

### What Clothes?

Have the children look closely at the pictures to see what the clothing looked like. Have them tell which pieces are similar to what they wear and which are different.

### Where Is Home?

What is Nadia's house like? Draw it. Draw yours. Label them.

# Africa

Appiah, S. (1988). *Amoko and Efua Bear*. New York: Macmillan Publishing Company. (Ages 4-7).

This story of a five-year-old girl in Ghana in West Africa tells of her love for her teddy bear, Efua, which she gave her own middle name. Efua goes everywhere with Amoko and eventually gets lost, injured, and repaired.

## Discussion Questions

1. What types of things does Amoko do with Efua?
2. Do you have a teddy bear? What name did you give it? Why?
3. What would have happened if Amoko's father had not found Efua?
4. What things did Amoko do with her mother? With her father?

# Classroom Activities

### Stew of Mutton and Yams

Amoko's father makes a stew of mutton and yams. To duplicate something similar, brown some lamb in a pan with a little oil. Chop vegetables. Add the vegetables to the lamb and cover with water. Thicken later. Bake the yams separately. Slice the yams lengthwise to make a dipper to dip into the stew. Give each child a separate dish.

Other stories tell of eating stew in this way. See *The Village of Round and Square Houses* and *Ashanti to Zulu*.

### Hide and Seek

A game the children play in this book is Hide and Seek. Review the rules with the children and play Hide and Seek in the classroom. Make the rules so that there is no running for base.

### Teddy Bear Day

Ask each child to bring a teddy bear to school and a long scarf to tie it to his back. He should show his teddy bear, tell about it, and then have it tied to his back for the day. Read *Corduroy* or *A Pocket for Corduroy*.

At the end of the day the bear and the child together can write about their adventures.

### Balance It on Your Head

At the market, several people are carrying bowls of food on their heads. Don't have the children try to carry bowls of food on their heads, but a chalkboard eraser is something to try. Give each child one of something similar and have him carry it around on his head for half a day.

# Hawaii

Bannon, L. (1961). *The Gift of Hawaii*. Chicago: Albert Whitman & Company. (Ages 4-7).

John John's mother has a birthday. Father brings her a big watermelon. They eat it all, but John John says his mother still has some birthday left. He heads to town with his pennies to buy her a gift only to find he has too few pennies to buy his mama a big gift. On the way home he makes her a lei. Mama loves it.

## Discussion Questions

1. What were some things John John wanted to give his mama for her birthday?
2. What different things can children give their moms for birthdays?
3. From the pictures that you saw, how would you know this story was about Hawaii?
4. What things in Hawaii are the same as where you live? What things in Hawaii are different from where you live?

## Classroom Activities

### Small, Medium and Large

Bring in boxes of clothes and shoes for the children to sort. Have them sort them into small, medium and large sizes. Older children can measure the length of the clothing and shoes to determine which stacks they belong in.

Label the clothes with the sizes small, medium and large. Set up a store where children can buy the clothes to use in the housekeeping center.

### Leis

Set out nut cups or cupcake cups for the children to make flowers. Glue two of them together to make a flower, bottom to bottom. Put one dab of perfume in the bottom of each cup. Each child should make several flowers. Let them dry for the day.

String the flowers onto yarn using a darning needle. Make it long enough to go around an adult's head. Take it home as a gift at the end of the day–or unit.

*Mom wearing the lei I made in school.*

### Muumuu Shop

Muumuus are the simple design that children usually make for their first clothing that they draw onto people. Give each child a piece of construction paper of a bright color. Have him cut a muumuu shape or trace around one that you have made. Let each child design his own muumuu with bright construction paper flowers. Place on a bulletin board entitled "The Muumuu Shop."

GA1431

# Mexico

Bannon, L. (1939). *Manuela's Birthday*. Chicago: Albert Whitman & Company. (Ages 4-7).

This birthday story is based on a true experience of the author's when she was living in a small Mexican village.

## Discussion Questions

1. Why was Manuela happy about the birthday gift she received from her friend?
2. What is your most memorable birthday gift?
3. How do you decide what it is that you want for your birthday?
4. What are all the things that Manuela did to celebrate her birthday?

## Classroom Activities

### Handmade Dolls

The children can make crying dolls from scraps of material or men's handkerchiefs. Place a wadded tissue in the center. Wind the material around it. Tie to make the head and neck.

Spread out the remaining material. Cut it in half from the bottom to within 3" (7.62 cm) of the neck. Spread out each half. Cut those from the outside to within 2" (5.08 cm) of the center of the material. Tie each of the four parts to make arms and legs. Faces can be drawn or glued on.

### Pinatas

Pinatas can be purchased in many party and paper stores. However, children will enjoy making their own.

Give each child a large balloon, blown up. Cover the balloon with strips of newspaper and a papier-mâché paste. Make the newspaper thick enough that none of the balloon shows through. On the final layer, use white newsprint.

Let these dry over the weekend. Stick a pin in to pop the balloon. Paint them with bright colors–yellow, turquoise, red, etc. Let this dry. Cut off the top or cut a hole in the side in order to put candy in each one. Children will probably not want to smash theirs with a stick. Instead, they can take them home filled with treats.

GA1431

# Asian

Behrens, J. (1965). *Soo Ling Finds a Way*. San Carlos, CA: Golden Gate Junior Books. (Ages 6-9).

Soo Ling is saddened when a modern laundromat opens across the street from her grandfather's laundry. She persuades her grandfather to iron in front of the large window in his laundry so that people going to the new laundromat will see how well he irons clothes. The owner of the new laundromat watches Soo Ling's grandfather iron, and he asks him to become his new partner. His new machines can wash people's clothes, and Mr. Soo can iron them.

## Discussion Questions

1. Why was Soo Ling sad when the new laundromat opened across the street from her grandfather's laundry?
2. Why was Soo Ling so happy at the end of the story?
3. What might have happened if Mr. Lee had not asked Soo Ling's grandfather to be his partner?

## Classroom Activities

### Sorting Laundry

Children love to sort laundry. It is much more meaningful than sorting beads. Bring in your own laundry–towels, socks, washcloths, etc. Let the children sort and fold the laundry.

Send a note home after the children get proficient with the laundry suggesting that the children sort the laundry for their parents.

### Things to Do with Grandfather

Give each child a piece of paper to fold in half. Ask him to draw a picture of his grandfather on one half. Use cotton for the white hair if his grandfather has white hair. On the other half have him make a list of things that he likes to do with his grandfather.

### Working in Pairs

In the story, two people get together. One is good at one thing. The other is good at another. Set up a task for the children to do where two children work together. One is good at one thing; the other is good at another thing.

### Washing with a Washboard

Bring a washboard into the classroom and let the children wash the dress-up clothes using a bucket of water and a washboard.

# Hispanic

Belpre, P. (1969). *Santiago*. New York: Frederick Warne and Company, Inc. (Ages 6-9).

Santiago has a pet chicken at his grandmother's in Puerto Rico. How can he get his friends in New York to believe him? With help from a parking lot chicken and a walking trip to the river for lunch, he succeeds.

### Discussion Questions

1. Why wouldn't Santiago's friends believe he had a pet chicken?
2. How did Santiago feel about his pet chicken?
3. Do you have something special at your grandmother's that you cannot bring home? Tell us about it.

## Classroom Activities

### At My Grandmother's House

Give each child a square piece of paper to fold into four boxes. In each box have him draw something from his grandmother's house. Cover the sheet with a piece of construction paper the same size, taping the tops together. Have the child decorate the construction paper as a house and put a roof on it. The house should lift up so you can see what is at his grandmother's house.

### My Friend's House

In a study of neighborhoods, it is fun to take a walk to see where each child lives. If you are in a neighborhood school, this is still possible to do. Pack lunches and go on a day when it is nice. Notify each parent that you will be there.

Have the children take along a stack of 6" (15.24 cm) square pieces of paper stapled together. On each have him write/draw something that makes each child's house special.

### Stereoscope

Seek a stereoscope for the children to examine. Some parents/grandparents may have one. Or try the local historical museum.

### Best Friends

Santiago and Ernie are best friends. Have the children make body-sized pictures of themselves with their best friends–not necessarily people in the room. On butcher paper, trace around two children holding hands or with their arms around each other's shoulders. Color or paint the bodies over two to three days. Post in the halls–Best Friends. (Children can write about what best friends do together.)

# Native American

Blood, C.L., and Link, M. (1976, 1990). *The Goat in the Rug by Geraldine.* New York: Aladdin Books, Macmillan Publishing Company. (Ages 4-7).

Geraldine the goat tells about living with Glenmae and having her wool made into a Navajo rug. The weaver's tools are pictured and the process of rugmaking from goat to rug are shown.

## Discussion Questions

1. How did Geraldine feel when she saw the scissors?
2. How did Glenmae make the rug?
3. What do you think Glenmae will do with the rug?
4. What would you do with the rug if you had it?

## Classroom Activities

### Weaving Geraldine

Give children pieces of brown paper with slits for weaving. Provide them with strips of black, red and white. They can make patterns or just weave colors. Older children may actually try to make two different colors in one line by tearing the strip off on the back and taping it in place on the back. Visit a weaver to watch something being woven. The children will be like Geraldine, sitting and watching–it does take a long time.

### What's a Rug For?

Give each child a piece of white paper to make into a rug like one that he has at home. Fray the ends if desired.

On the back of the rug, have him write/tell about how the rug is used, where it is placed and why he thinks it is where it is.

### Dye with the Flowers

Glenmae goes out looking for flowers to use as dye. Of course, Geraldine ate them all. Children can paint and dye with flowers.

Collect dandelions and let each child smear color onto a piece of paper. A fine line black outline around the yellow can make the outline of a picture of a dandelion.

Boiling flowers in water with vinegar will allow you to get a dye. Children can dye pieces of muslin to make bookmarks.

GA1431

# India

Bonnici, P. (1985). *The Festival*. Minneapolis: Carolrhoda Books, Inc. (Ages 4-7).

Arjuna, a small boy, was bored visiting his grandmother. However, this time it was different. He watched as each family member got ready for the festival. His mother gave him his first lungi, and he was allowed to sit with the men at the festival. He danced with them, but his lungi came undone and fell off. He was swept off of his feet by his uncle and went to listen to stories. On the way home he remembered that the headman had said that he was among the best dancers that evening.

## Discussion Questions

1. Why do you think Arjuna was bored when he went to his grandmother's house?
2. What things did Arjuna do at the festival?
3. What are some things you do when you go visit your grandparents?

## Classroom Activities

### A Visit with Grandmother

Arjuna has gone to his grandmother's for a visit. He stares at a lizard, picks berries but is bored until the festival comes. Fold a piece of paper into three boxes. Have each child draw his grandmother in one of the boxes. In the other two, have him draw pictures of things he does when he goes to visit his grandmother.

On the back, have him draw Arjuna's grandmother in one of the boxes. In the other two have him draw things that Arjuna does at his grandmother's.

### Mango Leaves

To decorate for the festival, Arjuna's mother hangs garlands of mango leaves over the doors and windows. Tie a rope from one chair to another. Have the children clothespin leaves to the rope. Tape the rope around the door frame as a decoration.

### Purple Berry Stains

Arjuna ends up with purple berry stains on his hands. For a snack, have the children eat blueberries, raspberries, and blackberries. When they are finished, examine their hands. Have them try to wash the stains off. (Assure them that they will come off with time–and a lot of soap.)

### Powdered Drawings

For one of the celebrations in India, powdered drawings are made on the front steps. Let children make drawings with powder (salt or sand will do). Color the powder with some dry tempera. Place glue on the paper. Shake the powder on the glue and let it dry.

# Native American: Pawnee (Skidi)

Cohen, C.L. (1988). *The Mud Pony*. New York: Scholastic, Inc. (Ages 6-9).

A young boy wants so much to have a pony like the other boys in his band. He molds one of clay which comes to life to guide him as he becomes chief. The horse, a part of Mother Earth, reminds the boy that Mother Earth will take care of him.

## Discussion Questions

1. Why did the boy want a horse?
2. How did he get a horse?
3. How did he feel when his band moved away and left him behind?
4. What did he do when he couldn't find his mother and father?

## Classroom Activities

### Mud Ponies

Give the children play dough and let them shape mud ponies from the "clay." An examination of horses will help. Feathers may be placed along the mane for decoration.

### Tepees

The family of the boy traveled to find the buffalo and lived in tepees. Children can examine the shape of a tepee and make a small one for themselves. A snowcone cup turned upside down should be painted a buckskin color. If you have no cups, make a cone from construction paper and paint it. Let it dry. Indian designs or symbols from this book may be copied in black onto the "tepee."
Cut a flap for the door.

### All Alone

The boy found himself all alone. List some of the things he did? What do you do when you are all alone? List some of the things that you do.

### Mother Earth

The pony kept telling the boy that Mother Earth could help him. What types of things do we get from Mother Earth?
Draw pictures of things that come from the earth. Cut them out. Glue them onto brown paper. Title the picture "From Mother Earth."
There are other stories in this book that talk about conservation. Try *Brother Eagle, Sister Sky* and *The Legend of the Palm Tree*.

GA1431

## European America, Barbados, Puerto Rico, Vietnam, India, China, Haiti

Dooley, N. (1991). *Everybody Cooks Rice*. Minneapolis: Carolrhoda Books, Inc. (Ages 4-7).

Carrie goes out to find her younger brother for dinner. She checks the different homes in the neighborhood only to find each having rice for dinner. She returns home to rice for dinner herself. All recipes for the meals are included at the end of the book.

### Discussion Questions

1. How did the families in the story serve and eat rice?
2. Which rice sounded best to you? Why?
3. What is your favorite way to eat rice?
4. How is rice cooked?

## Classroom Activities

### Rice Recipes

Write each of the recipes at the end of the book on a recipe card. Post these in a writing center with a stack of recipe cards–larger ones for smaller children. Children can copy the recipes during free play or writing center time.

Send home a recipe card to the parents with a note attached asking for their favorite recipe that uses rice. Place four of these at a time on a copy machine. Copy them. Let the children cut them out and staple together to make a Rice Recipe Book.

### Feast of Rice

Ask four to six of your parents to provide a rice dish for a Feast of Rice. Place the dishes on separate tables with the rice recipe on the table. Give each child a sectioned plate. Have him select one rice recipe at a time to sample, being sure to pick up a rice recipe card at the table while he is getting served. When he has finished, have him draw a happy face, medium face or sad face on the card to indicate how well he liked the recipe.

*Rice and Mushroom Casserole*

Tally the results later in class, being sure not to hurt the feelings of the parents or children whose parents fixed the dishes.

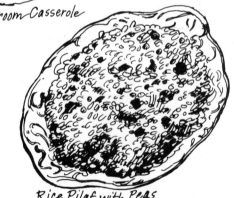

*Rice Pilaf with Peas*

### What Is It?

Examine the different kinds and sizes of rice. Use a magnifying glass. Describe each.

# Haiti

Dorbin, A. (1973). *Josephine's 'magination: A Tale of Haiti.* New York: Scholastic, Inc. (Ages 6-9).

Josephine's mother makes brooms to take to market. Josephine goes with her mother and shops while her mother sells the broom. She finds a doll she wants. She is given a straw toy by a man who has made it from his 'magination. Josephine returns home and uses her mother's scraps to make a broom doll. She and her mother take them to town, and they sell quite well.

## Discussion Questions

1. What do Josephine and her mother do together?
2. How does Josephine's family earn money for food and shelter?
3. How did Josephine make the doll?
4. If you had to make a toy out of scraps at your house, what could you use?

## Classroom Activities

### The Balancing Act

Josephine and her mom carry things to town on their heads. Just how easy is that? Let the children try. Start with small things that are not slippery. Advance to larger things that have some resistance to their base. Children enjoy the challenge.

### Around the Head

In most of the pictures of this book, Josephine has a scarf around her head. She also makes a scarf for around the head of the doll that she makes.

Place some easy-wash scarves or large bandanas in the house area. Tie them around the children's heads for play. (Remember to wash each one after use on only one child.)

### A Penny to Spend

Josephine had but a few pennies to spend. Just what will a penny buy? At a store nearby, pick up enough penny items so that you have one for each child in your class. Put these in a bowl. Also put out several other things that are more expensive.

Give each child a penny and see if he knows what things cost a penny by allowing him to buy anything that actually costs a penny.

### Flower Dolls

Josephine describes how she makes flower dolls by using a large flower, sticking a stick through the flower to the stem, and putting a face on the top part of the stick.

Provide flowers for the children to make flower dolls.

# Hispanic

Ets, M.H. (1963). *Gilberto and the Wind*. New York: Viking Press. (Ages 4-7).

The story of Gilberto is a simple one of investigating all the things that the wind can do. Gilberto relies on the wind for several activities (sailing his boat, flying his kite, making his pinwheel turn, getting his apple down from the tree, carrying away his bubbles). He is also disappointed when the wind breaks his umbrella, takes away his balloon, blows the leaves from the trees. When the wind dies down, Gilberto falls asleep.

## Discussion Questions

1. What are some fun things that Gilberto does with the wind?
2. What are some things the wind did that made Gilberto sad?
3. What are some things you know that the wind can do?

## Classroom Activities

### The Wind and Pinwheels

Each child needs one square of paper, scissors, an unsharpened pencil and a straight pin. Fold the square to make a triangle. Fold it once more. Open. Place a quarter in the center. Trace around it. Put a dot in the center. Have the children cut from each corner of the square on the fold line to the circle made by the quarter. Stick a pin in each corner, progressing around the square sequentially from corner to corner. Finally, place the pin into the center of the circle and stick the whole pinwheel into the eraser of a pencil. Find out what the wind does to the pinwheel.

### Pinwheel Bulletin Board

On both sides of a giant square of paper draw things the wind can do. Make it into a giant pinwheel for the bulletin board.

### Bubbles

Provide the children with different shapes of bubble blowers and "bubble stuff." Blow the bubbles in the room and try to catch them. When it is windy out one day, take the children outdoors and let the wind blow the bubbles. Once again, try to catch them.

### Raking the Leaves

Rake leaves into a pile and jump into them. Older children can come along and bag them later. Daring teachers will even bring in green leaves and put them out in the room for the children to rake.

### Balloon Activities

(Try these indoors and then try them outside on a windy day.)
Batting balloons, tossing balloons, controlling balloons

# Chinese

Flack, M., and Wiese, K., (1933, 1961). *The Story About Ping.* New York: Viking Press. (Ages 4-7).

This charming story about a small duck on the Yangtze River tells about his separation from his family, a near tragedy, and a reunion.

## Discussion Questions

1. How did Ping get lost from his family?
2. What made him try to find his family?
3. What do you suppose his mother and father did when he came back home?

## Classroom Activities

### "Six Little Ducks"

Six little ducks that I once knew
Fat ones, skinny ones, fair ones, too.
But the one little duck with the feather in his back
He led the others with a quack, quack, quack
Quack, quack, quack, quack, quack, quack
He led the others with a quack, quack, quack.

Sing or say the words to the song "Six Little Ducks" as children walk in line following the lead duck. Change *he* to *she* periodically.

### Dramatize the Story

The story of Ping is one that young children can easily remember. Review the sequence of the story with them first. Ask for a volunteer to be the boy, the family, the boat keeper, Ping, some ducks and some dark fishing birds.

As you or a child from the group read the story, have the children act out the parts. Change parts.

Simple costumes can be made. Duck feet for the ducks, wings for the birds and housekeeping dress-up clothes for the people.

### Lost

Ping gets lost, sleeps alone overnight, sets out to find his family and eventually gets reunited. This would be a good time to talk with children about what to do if they get lost. Follow the policies set up in your school and community when you present this to the children. If you do not have a school policy, it would be a good time to develop one.

# Japanese American

Friedman, I.R. (1984). *How My Parents Learned to Eat*. Boston: Houghton Mifflin Company. (Ages 4-7).

A delightful book about an American soldier who falls in love with a Japanese girl while his ship is in Japan. He is afraid to invite her out to eat because he cannot use chopsticks. She is afraid to go out to eat with him because she doesn't know how to use a knife and fork. Each learns the other's ways and their child then uses sometimes one, sometimes the other.

### Discussion Questions
1. Why did the little girl use both chopsticks and forks to eat?
2. What food did the lady use when learning to eat with a knife and fork?
3. How is it easiest for you to eat?

# Classroom Activities

### Eating Peas

Eating peas is difficult for everyone. Boil up a pot of frozen peas. (Have on hand some mashed potatoes.) Give each child a small bowl of peas, a pair of chopsticks, a fork and a spoon.

Ask each child to eat the peas with his fingers (quite acceptable in olden times), a spoon, a fork, and chopsticks. Give each a dab of mashed potatoes and have him use only chopsticks or a fork to eat the peas (mixed with potatoes, of course).

### Spooning Beans

In a fine motor center, place a large bowl of beans (or beads if you cannot use food), several smaller empty bowls, and some spoons. Have the children scoop the beans with the spoons into the smaller bowls and then back again.

### Serving the Meals

When you serve meals in your classroom, do it family style. Place serving bowls of the foods on the tables with serving spoons. Let the children spoon the servings onto their own plates.

### Using Good Manners

While eating with the children, encourage good manners at all meals, but focus on it periodically. Keep one hand in the lap to avoid pushing food onto utensils, napkins in laps and no blowing on food (stir or mix it to cool it). A good book to teach children how to mind their manners is *Soup Should Be Seen and Not Heard* (B. Brainard and S. Behr).

# Poland

Glasgow, A. (1971). *The Pair of Shoes.* New York: The Dial Press. (Ages 6-9).

This story tells of a poor Jewish family of five in Poland who had only one pair of shoes. The oldest boy wore the shoes until the father decided it was time for the other children to wear them. The young daughter wore them to town to buy a candle for the Friday night holy service. She broke her ankle on her return. Mother told the oldest son to wear the shoes to town, sell her prized possession, and get the doctor. The son returned with the doctor, money and the mother's prized possession. The shoes were gone. Only then did each child get his own pair of shoes.

## Discussion Questions

1. How did the family get the one pair of shoes?
2. Why didn't they have more than one pair of shoes?
3. If your family could have only one pair of shoes, which pair would you choose? Why?
4. When do you wear shoes? When do you go barefooted?

## Classroom Activities

### Shine Those Shoes

The children in our story took excellent care of the one pair of shoes their family had. Have your children shine shoes.

Place old shoes, shoe polish, shoe shining brushes, rags, newspapers, smocks, in a center. Demonstrate the process of polishing shoes to the children. Let them polish the shoes to their hearts' content.

### Barefooted

Let the children go barefooted in the classroom for the day and tell how the various parts of the room feel. If it is cold, have old rags made out of sheets for the children to wrap their feet in to keep them warm. Be careful about the rags being slippery.

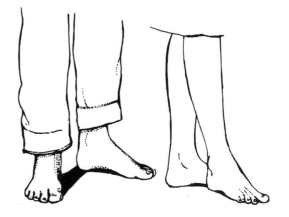

### Dubbie's Family and Mine

The family in this story consisted of a mother, a father, three children, four chickens and a cow. Place this family unit on a bulletin board. Title it "Dubbie's Family." Ask each child to draw a picture of his family unit and title with his own family's name. Compare and contrast the family units.

GA1431

# Native American

Goble, P. (1980). *The Gift of the Sacred Dog.* New York: Bradbury Press. (Ages 6-9).

Goble tells the story of how the horses used by the Native Americans were truly a gift from the Great Spirit. Another story about how the horses came is told in Yolen and Moser's *Sky Dogs*.

## Discussion Questions

1. How did the horses come to the people?
2. What did they use the horses for? Why were they important?
3. What types of things are horses used for today?

## Classroom Activities

### Decorated Horses

Examine a picture of a horse carefully with the children, showing them the four legs with their parts, the shape of the head with its parts, tail, mane, etc. Give each child a piece of paper on which to glue a construction paper horse he makes from cut pieces of construction paper. The main parts he should address are body, legs, neck and head. Onto those he glues mane, tail, hooves, ears, eyes, nose and mouth. Provide them glitter, ribbon, materials scraps, etc., with which to decorate the horse.

### Sunset

Goble illustrates a beautiful sunset. Have the children look at the picture. After a while, close the book and have them recall what they saw. Have each child glue on some mountainy shapes at the bottom of the page. He can then choose a color for the sun, cut out a large circle, and glue it going down behind the mountains–actually lifting up the piece of the mountain and glueing it down. From there he can make the sunset on the rest of the white paper.

# Sioux

Goble, P. (1990). *Iktomi and the Ducks*. New York: Bradbury Press. (Ages 6-9).

This story tells of Iktomi, the trickster, who goes in search of his horse, sees ducks he wants for dinner, tricks the ducks into death, gets caught by a tree, loses his ducks and sets off in search of the coyote who stole the ducks. Does he remember his horse?

## Discussion Questions

1. What were some of the "tricks" or "pranks" in this story?
2. Who played tricks besides Iktomi?
3. Were there good tricks and bad tricks? What were they?
4. How do you feel when people play tricks on you or tease you?

# Classroom Activities

### Retelling the Story

Place the children in five groups. Each group is assigned a "character" from the story to make Iktomi, his horse, ducks, the trees, the coyote. Provide them with large pieces of craft paper, construction paper, scissors, glue, crayons.

To retell the story, have one child from each group hold his "character" in front of the group. Read the story and have the children "act out" their parts. After many times of this, place the characters in an area where children may use them at will.

### True and Untrue

Some of the things in this story could happen, and some of them could not happen. It is difficult for young children to tell the difference. Go through the book and ask the children to tell you the episodes of real happenings and unreal happenings. What they might come up with will be like this:

| Real | Unreal |
|---|---|
| Iktomi went looking for his horse. | The ducks talked. |
| Iktomi saw ducks and wanted roast duck. | Iktomi makes the ducks dance with their eyes shut. |
| Iktomi gathered grass in his blanket. | Iktomi thumps ducks on head and kills them. |
| Iktomi walked with his blanket on his back. | The coyote buries red coals in place of the duck. |
| The blanket is full of songs. | |

### Take-Home Story

Give each child a strip of paper 6" x 18" (15.24 x 45.72 cm). Fold it into five boxes. Let the child draw the characters from the story in sequence on the folded pieces of paper and write a short sentence telling about each.

# South America

Gramatky, H. (1961). *Bolivar.* New York: G.P. Putnam's Sons. (Ages 6-9).

This book is the story of a young boy, Pepito, and his donkey, Bolivar, in the Andes Mountains of South America. The donkey, who was named for the famous hero of South America, Simon Bolivar, is always in trouble and the adults want to send him away. Pepito saves him and decides to show the people that Bolivar can work. Of course, nothing seems to go right for the pair. However, during the fiesta, the bull from the bullring escapes, and it is Bolivar to the rescue. A hero!

## Discussion Questions

1. What type of trouble did the donkey get into?
2. How did Bolivar save the day?
3. What problems would you have if you wanted to keep a donkey for a pet?

## Classroom Activities

### Heroes

Heroes abound in the world. Young children pick their heroes from many different sources. Discuss with the children why Bolivar is a hero.

Have them list other heroes that they know. Don't be discouraged if most of them come from Saturday morning cartoons. Each time, have the children tell you why they think the hero is a hero.

Make a hero chart.

List all the things that a hero does (according to the children).

> **A Hero**
>
> fights the bad guy
>
> saves lives
>
> wins awards
>
> good in sports

### Bulls for the Bullfight

A follow-up story to read to the children about bulls and bullfights is *Ferdinand*. Ferdinand doesn't want to fight. He just wants to smell the flowers.

### Community Celebrations

Pepito and Bolivar go to the fiesta in the village. It is a celebration for everyone. What celebrations are there in your community for everyone? Make a list of them. Put the family name of the child under each one that his family attends.

GA1431

# Western Hemisphere and Africa

Gray, N. (1988). *A Country Far Away*. New York: Orchard Books. (Ages 4-7).

Side-by-side pictures reveal many similarities between the lives of two boys, one living in a western country and the other living in an African village.

## Discussion Questions

1. How are the two boys' lives similar, yet different?
2. Do you think one family is happier than the other? Why or why not?
3. Why were they all riding the bus into the African town instead of taking the train? What was broken down in the Western country on that same page?

## Classroom Activities

### Chores

Have each student make a list of the ways he can help his parents around the house. The list might include taking out the trash, walking the dog, making his bed, washing or drying dishes, etc. From the student lists make a master list on the chalkboard and tally the number of students that does each listed chore.

### The Family Photograph

In both of these cultures the family was important. On a sheet of paper have each student list the names of all the people in his family, immediate and extended. Beside each name he should put how he is related. If he wants to draw a picture of each family member, let him.

### Playing

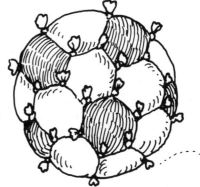

The African children made a soccer ball by tying material together. Ask students to think of games they have played that required them to make the materials for the game out of common objects found around the house. Let volunteers tell how these games were played and why they enjoyed playing these games.

### What You Do, What I Do

Have each of the children bring a picture in of one specific event: his first birthday would be a good choice. Place photos on bulletin board to show how they all do things a bit differently but somewhat the same.

GA1431

# Black American

Greenfield, E. (1976). *First Pink Light*. New York: Scholastic Book Services. (Ages 4-7).

Tyree plays near his mother while she does her homework. He attempts to delay going to bed in about as many ways as he can. He wants to wait up to see his daddy who has been away taking care of his grandmother. He's not due in until early morning (at first pink light). Mom and Tyree compromise. Dad comes home to find a sleeping Tyree and carries him to bed.

## Discussion Questions

1. Why did Tyree want to wait up?
2. What types of things do you do while you are waiting for your parents to come home?
3. Tyree's mom is doing homework at a table with a pencil and some books. What things does your family do at a table? With a pencil? With books?
4. How did Tyree's mom get him to go to sleep?

## Classroom Activities

### Sunrise

Take several photos of sunrises in the area where you live. Have the children examine them and tell how the sky looks in each of them.

Draw/Paint sunrises from these pictures on a large piece of white or brown butcher paper with thin tempera.

In order to show that they are sunrises, have the children draw on black pieces of paper things that happen in the morning, cut them out, attach them to the sunrise mural. Possibilities are a child getting out of bed, children walking to school, cars going to work, birds singing.

### Working with Pencils

What types of things can be written with pencils? Give each child a pencil and a piece of paper. Make all of the pieces of paper different shapes and relatively small. Try triangles, octagons, rectangles (long and short), squares (big and little). See what meaningful things they write on them during the day.

At the end of the day, collect the writings and have the children tell the group about what they wrote. (Accept all types of writing, listening carefully to what the children tell you they wrote.)

### Card Table Tents

Bring a card table into the room with several sheets, books, etc., and let the children make a card table tent to play in.

GA1431

# Black American

Havill, J. (1989). *Jamaica Tag-Along*. Boston: Houghton Mifflin Company. (Ages 4-7).

Jamaica likes her older brother, but he refuses to let her tag along with him and his friends. So Jamaica goes off by herself and allows a younger child to play with her. In an earlier book, *Jamaica's Find*, Jamaica finds a lost toy.

### Discussion Questions

1. Why did Jamaica want to tag along with her brother Ossie?
2. Do you have an older brother or sister? Does he/she like it when you tag along with him/her? Why do you think he/she feels that way?
3. What lesson did Jamaica learn when Betro wanted to help build the sand castle?

## Classroom Activities

### Being Kind

Talk to your class about the importance of being a good example to those around us, especially younger people. Arrange for your class to spend some play time with a younger class. Your class could plan some games for the playground or an art/craft project that is appropriate for the age of the children they are going to have in their class.

Mrs. Roberts Kindergarten class visited our class. A little boy named Tony became my friend. I helped him a lot.

### Watching and Waiting

Ask an older class to do something with your class. First take the children to watch the older children doing something–playing soccer, singing, reading, etc. Then have the older group do things with the younger ones.

### Cooperation

Discuss with your class the importance of cooperating when you are trying to accomplish something as a group. Identify a class project, such as building a village in the sandpile or drawing and painting a mural.

Help your class decide how they will do the project and what job(s) each person will have. Supervise closely and encourage cooperation as they complete the project.

by Mrs. Schraber's class

GA1431

# Black American

Howard, Chats E.F. (1991). *Aunt Flossie's Hat (and Crab Cakes Later)*. New York: Houghton Mifflin Company. (Ages 4-7).

Two young girls go to visit their great-great Aunt Flossie who serves tea and cookies while the girls try on all of Aunt Flossie's hats. Aunt Flossie tells her memories as the girls model.

## Discussion Questions

1. Where do you go when you wear hats?
2. What types of hats do you wear?
3. Where did Aunt Flossie wear hats?
4. Where do you get to go with adults when they ask you to act in a grown-up way?

# Classroom Activities

### What's in the Box?

Bring in several boxes to the classroom, each filled with something of interest to young children. Be sure there are enough boxes so each group of four children can have one. Separate them into groups of four and let them examine in private what is in their box. Have them decide on one clue for the others and have them try to guess what is in their box.

Put two of the groups of children together. Have each group try to figure out what is in the other's box.

### Hat Boxes

Bring in a hat box to show the children what one is. In the box have a hat. Show the children what you look like in the hat.

Make a 10" (25.4 cm) piece of waxed paper for each child. When each tries on the hat he must first place the waxed paper on his head (to protect from lice), and then place that hat on the waxed paper. Have a mirror nearby.

### Hats Tell Stories

Bring in several hats that are familiar to the children. Have each one tell about what happened the day it was worn.

### Floating Hats

Use the water table and let the children try to float some old hats. Place things in the hats to see if they will act as boats.

GA1431

# Italy

Hughes, M. (1967). *Why Carlo Wore a Bonnet*. New York: Lothrop, Lee & Shepard Co., Inc. (Ages 4-7).

Carlo was usually the best donkey in all of Italy. However, when a fly buzzed in his ear, he became as bad as all other donkeys. Grandmother made him a bonnet for his ears, and he was as good as ever.

## Discussion Questions

1. What type of work did Carlo do?
2. How did Grandmother and Giorgio work together?
3. Where do you suppose Giorgio's parents were?
4. Why do people wear hats?

# Classroom Activities

## Safety

Be sure to warn the children not to blow in each other's ears or into the ears of animals.

## Donkey Hats

Give each child a paper plate, a strip of paper and some construction paper to construct a hat for a donkey. When children are all finished, tie each bonnet onto each child. Have the children look into a mirror as the donkey did, and have a donkey hat parade.

## Up the Wrong Sleeve

Grandmother tries to put her sweater over the donkey's ears. It doesn't work. Have the children try putting sweaters on themselves or on others in ways that are different from the way they are to wear them. Check them out in the mirror for a good laugh.

## Listen to the Flies Buzz

Try to capture some flies and keep them in a jar for a day. Let the children put their ears to the air holes in the bug catcher and listen to the flies buzz.

## Being Stubborn

Talk with the children about things they don't mind doing and things they don't like to do. Make a list of each. Grandmother made the donkey feel better, and then he didn't mind doing the things he didn't want to do. Have the children tell you what would make them feel more like doing what they don't like to do.

## Related Stories

Read *Why Mosquitoes Buzz in People's Ears* and do the activities suggested.

# Japan

Isami, I. (1989). *The Fox's Egg*. Minneapolis: Carolrhoda Books, Inc. (Ages 4-7).

A fox finds an egg but decides it would be tastier after it was hatched. Sitting on the egg to hatch it makes the fox feel protective and presents some unexpected problems.

## Discussion Questions

1. Why didn't the fox eat the egg?
2. What have you found? Who did it belong to? What did you do with it?
3. Why do you think the fox became so protective of the chick?
4. What do you think happened as the chick grew up?

## Classroom Activities

### Hatching Eggs

For those of you who are brave, try hatching eggs in an incubator. Time the arrival of the chicks for a Tuesday and use several eggs. At various stages of development you can see the changing status of the embryo through a strong light.

### Concentration

Make a set of egg-shaped cards with a mother and its baby animal on one side and blank on the other side. Put the children at a table with a chart showing which adult belongs with which baby. Have them spend a week or so matching the animals. When they can do this with little difficulty, have them place the cards on the floor, picture-side down, and play Concentration, matching adults to children.

### The Fox's Chick

Give each child a large yellow pom-pom, a pair of googly eyes, and a small orange triangle. Glue the googly eyes onto the yellow pom-pom and add the orange triangle for the beak.

Give each child a long piece of nest-colored yarn to wad up for a nest.

Two similar books are *Are You My Mother?* and *Horton Hatches a Who*.

GA1431

# Black American

Keats, E.J. (1969). *Goggles.* New York: Young Readers Press, Inc. (Ages 4-7).

This story is about two young boys who have a hideout. One finds a pair of motorcycle goggles and puts them on. A group of big boys comes along and demands the goggles. The boys refuse to give them up. The big boys knock one of the boys down and the goggles go flying. The dog picks them up and they all head for the hideout, going different directions. Eventually they trick the big boys and sit on the front porch looking at the world through the goggles.

## Discussion Questions

1. What did the boys do with the goggles that they found?
2. How do you think the goggles got lost in the first place?
3. Who do you think they might have belonged to?
4. How do you think it would feel to wear motorcycle goggles?

## Classroom Activities

### All Types of Goggles

Young children love to try on various types of goggles and glasses. Place several different kinds (unbreakable) in the housekeeping area or in a box near a mirror. Try various kinds and sizes including motorcycle goggles, glasses, dark glasses, swimming goggles.

### Me and My Goggles

After the children have had time to try on the various kinds and sizes of goggles, have each choose the one he likes best and photograph each wearing the goggles. Ask him to tell you about what he would be or do in the goggles. Record the response or have each write the story himself. Post them on a bulletin board made of a giant pair of goggles.

CHRISTINA ROBERTSON

### Through the Pipe

Archie and Peter look through the pipe to see the big boys. Get a piece of 1" (2.54 cm) plumber's pipe for the children to look through. Have them focus on one thing and draw what they see on round paper.

### Hideout

Provide children with these materials: sheets, blankets, a space, signs, markers. Let them build a hideout.

Other Keats' books include *Whistle for Willie, The Snowy Day, Peter's Chair, Pet Show, Louie, Hi Cat, A Letter for Amy.*

# Native American

Krensky, Stephen. (1991). *Children of the Earth and Sky*. New York: Scholastic, Inc. (Ages 6-9).

Native American children were trained to help their families at early ages. Skills such as hunting or weaving were not hobbies or games; they were important parts of everyday life. This book includes five stories about the experiences of Hopi, Comanche, Mohican, Navajo, and Mandan children. The children are imaginary, but the stories give the reader a range and variety of Native American experiences.

## Discussion Questions
1. Which tribes moved their homes from place to place? Why did they move?
2. Which tribes stayed in one place? Why were they able to stay there?
3. Why do people move today?

## Classroom Activities

### Clay Pots
After reading the story "A Hopi Potter," give each child some clay and let him make a clay pot. The pot can then be dried and glazed and baked in a kiln. If a kiln is not available, substitute modeling clay and let the children decorate the clay pots by drawing designs in the modeling clay with a pencil with a dull point.

### Paper Kachinas
Display some kachina dolls and/or some pictures of kachina dolls in the classroom. Give the children some construction paper and let them draw and color kachina dolls using crayons or markers. These can then be cut out and colored on the back side of the paper dolls. Attach a piece of string or thread to the dolls and hang them from the lights or ceiling.

### Friendly Calls
After reading "A Comanche Rider," divide the class into four groups. Choose two of the groups to be part of the Comanche tribe and two to belong to another tribe. Separate the two tribes by letting one go into another room or, at least, into the hallway. Each child in the group should decide on a call (noise) that would tell the other children in the tribe who he is without the tribe seeing or talking to him. After they have practiced and learned the calls of their tribe members, bring them into the classroom. Place one group from each tribe in one half of the room and the other group from each tribe in the other side of the room. Use some obstruction, for example, room divider, bookcase, sheet, to prevent the children on one side from seeing the children on the other side. One at a time each child should make his call three times and the children on the other side have to identify which tribe that call is from.

GA1431

# Cambodia

Lee, J.M. (1991). *Silent Lotus*. New York: Farrah, Straus, & Giroux. (Ages 4-7).

This story tells of a young girl in Cambodia who was unable to speak because she could not hear. Her parents find ways to communicate with her. She loves to watch the herons, cranes and white egrets and walk as they walk.

Her parents take her to the temple in the city where Lotus sees dancers. She feels the vibrations of the drums and cymbals and moves like the dancers move. A graceful old woman teaches Lotus to dance the tales of gods and kings.

## Discussion Questions

1. Why could Lotus not speak?
2. Why did she like to be with the herons, cranes and white egrets?
3. Why did the parents take Lotus to the temple?
4. What other types of things do you think Lotus could do? What couldn't she do?

## Classroom Activities

### Walk as They Walk

Have the children take a walk outside to look at various animals and birds and see how they walk. Look closely at each animal or bird. After a while, ask the children to show you exactly how each walks.

Take a trip to the zoo to watch other animals, especially the ones mentioned in the story if they are there. Let the children try these animal walks, too.

When they have learned the walks well, have them play charades. One child pretends to be one animal, the others guess.

### Talking with Your Hands

Children are encouraged through many different television shows to learn to sign. Older children can learn the alphabet and sign their names and names of friends when they choose teams, get in line, go to lunch, etc. They can also sign their spelling words.

Younger children might learn letters but can learn words, songs, and actions as well. Many good books for children are available.

### Telling Stories with No Words

The children know many stories and nursery rhymes. Ask one child to try to tell the children a story without using any words and have the other children guess what the story is. Do it as long as the children feel comfortable, requesting only those who feel comfortable "telling" the stories.

GA1431

# Black American

Lewin, H. (1983). *Jafta*. Minneapolis: Carolrhoda Books, Inc. (Ages 4-7).

Jafta is a story about a young boy who talks about what he does when he is happy, tired, and cross. In addition he talks about being strong, tall, long, and fast. Each time, he tells about being as "fast" as an animal.

## Discussion Questions

1. What does Jafta do when he is cross?
2. What types of things do you think make him cross?
3. If you could be as tall as something, what would you like to be as tall as?

## Classroom Activities

### As Tall As

Divide a sheet of paper into three parts, making them long and tall parts. At the top of each part write "As Tall As." Ask the children to draw pictures of tall things in each of the boxes, allowing them to use as many sheets of paper as they want. When they are all finished, each child can cut his own out and make a book out of them to read to his friends, teachers, and parents.

### I Can

Ask the children to name as many animals as they can. Put the names of these animals on a piece of chart paper at the far right side as the children tell them to you.

After the list of animals is complete, ask the children to tell you something that the animals do–hop, run, fly, etc. Record in front of the animal: "Runs like a horse."

Ask the children to choose one or two to complete with the total sentence–I can _____ like a _____. When they have written the sentence, have them illustrate both themselves and the animal doing what they have written about.

### Sort the Animals

Collect pictures of animals, mount on index cards, and label.

Ask the children to list words that describe animals–big, little, wild, tame, etc. Write each word on a separate index card.

Place the index cards and the animal pictures in a center. Ask the child to choose one index card to put on the table, sort through the pictures, and place all the animals that the word describes below the word. At the top of a long strip of paper write the word. At the bottom, illustrate each animal and write its name.

Other *Jafta* books include *Jafta's Father, Jafta's Mother, Jafta–The Town, Jafta–The Journey.*

GA1431

# Eskimo

Luenn, N. (1990). *Nessa's Fish*. New York: Atheneum. (Ages 4-7).

This story tells how Nessa's ingenuity and bravery saves from a fox, wolves, and a bear the fish that she and her grandmother caught to feed everyone in their Eskimo camp.

## Discussion Questions

1. How did Nessa and her grandmother fish in the lake when it was frozen?
2. How did Nessa solve her problem about being alone in a dangerous place and having to take care of her sick grandmother?
3. Have you ever been in danger? What did you do?

## Classroom Activities

### A Play About Nessa

Change this story into a play and assign parts to your students. Nessa, the grandmother, a fox, wolves, a bear, the grandfather, her father and mother, the other villagers and their dogs are the play's characters. Read the story to your class several times until they know the story line. Let them use their words for the play's dialogue.

### Grandmother and Me

Have students write or tell a story about something they did with their grandmothers. For those children without grandmothers, they can substitute other older persons. Have them draw pictures to illustrate the story.

### Going Fishing

Give the children several pieces of white paper and let them outline and then paint fish on them. Each fish should be about the size of the piece of paper. After they finish the fish and let them dry, cut them out. Put a paper clip on the nose of each or a piece of magnetic tape on the back. Make a fishing pole with a magnet on one end.

Place the fish on the floor. Place a large box over them and put a hole in the top (which is the bottom of the box). Let the children fish in pairs.

After all the fish are out of the lake, have each child line his fish up in order, smallest to largest. Count each set of fish. Graph the different colors of fish.

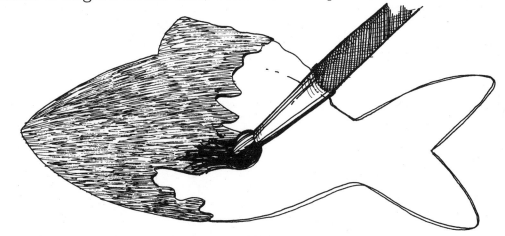

# Puerto Rico

Martel, C. (1976). *Yagua Days*. New York: The Dial Press. (Ages 6-9).

Adan's family came from Puerto Rico to live in New York where his parents had a small store where they sold vegetables. Adan, now a city boy, was convinced that these fruits and vegetables grew in trucks. During one summer, the family returned to Puerto Rico where Adan not only helped pick the fruits and vegetables, but enjoyed the trip down the slippery grass on a yagua (much like a Slip and Slide) to the river below.

## Discussion Questions

1. Why did Adan think that fruits and vegetables grew on trucks?
2. Where do fruits and vegetables grow? How do you know?
3. What fun things do you do when it rains?
4. What are some different ways you can get into a swimming place?

# Classroom Activities

### Food for Thought

Bring in several pieces of fruit or different vegetables. Ask the children where they think these things grow. Categorize the fruits and vegetables by where/how the children think they grow.

Older children can check the encyclopedias for the "right" answers. You will need to model looking up the information for the younger children and show them the answers that are found in books.

Recategorize the food.

### Bodega

Give each child a piece of brown paper to serve as a box for his fruit/vegetable. Let each child then choose a different fruit or vegetable to make from construction paper. Have them make several pieces of the fruit/vegetable and place them attractively onto the box." (See the pictures in the book for examples.) Place these on a bulletin board entitled "Bodega."

### Learning the Language

This book provides a dictionary at the back telling how to pronounce each of the Spanish words and giving a definition. Post some of the more frequently used ones in the room to encourage the children to use throughout the day.

# Native American

Martin, Jr., B., and Archambault, J. (1966, 1987). *Knots on a Counting Rope.* New York: Henry Holt and Company. (Ages 6-9).

Boy-Strength-of-Blue-Horses, a young blind Indian boy, and his grandfather reminisce about his birth, his first horse, and an exciting horse race.

## Discussion Questions

1. How did the young boy get his name?
2. What are the dark mountains he has to cross?
3. Why does the boy feel strong when he is with his grandfather?

## Classroom Activities

### Knots on a Counting Rope

Choose a story that your students would be able to memorize. Read or tell this story to them. After each reading or telling, tie a knot in a piece of rope. Encourage your students to tell or read the story when they feel able to do it. When all have read or told the story, start over with a new story and a new piece of rope.

### When I Was Born

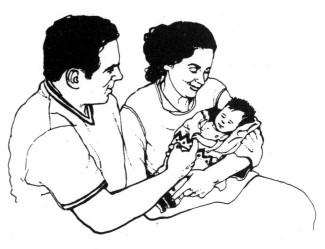

Send a note home asking the parents to tell their child the story of when he/she was born. They should include the time of day or night, the place of birth, the weather conditions, conversations surrounding the birth, unusual happenings, etc. These stories can be retold by the children in school. Have a rope with knots in it and let each child hold this rope while he/she tells the story surrounding his/her birth.

### Grandfathers

Boy-Strength-of-Blue-Horses had a special relationship with his grandfather. His grandfather told him stories, taught him to ride a horse, encouraged him, and helped him appreciate his abilities. Discuss this relationship with your children. Give each a piece of paper and ask him to fold it in half and then in half again, so that his paper is divided in quarters. With the paper opened, ask them to draw or write something that describes one of his grandfathers in each box. Children who want to share stories about their grandfathers should be encouraged to do so.

GA1431

# Japan

Martin, P.M. (1968). *Kumi and the Pearl*. New York: G.P. Putnam's Sons. (Ages 6-9).

The story tells of a young girl who wants to be a diving girl. However, she is left to care for her baby sister who cannot yet walk. Her grandfather tells her he will teach her to dive when her baby sister can walk. She finds a friend who wants to play with her sister while she teaches herself to hold her breath for longer and longer periods of time. When her grandfather falls into the water, she has to use her skill to loosen the pole that holds his foot. He allows her to dive with the diving girls the next day.

## Discussion Questions

1. Why wouldn't Grandfather let Kumi dive for oysters?
2. What types of things do you think Kumi did to entertain her younger sister?
3. What kind of a job do you think Kumi will do when she grows up?
4. Do you ever have to take care of your sisters or brothers? Why or why not?

# Classroom Activities

## Pearls in Oysters

Let the children make a paper oyster with a pearl inside. Give each child a piece of creamy paper and have him cut out two shell shapes the same size. Tape together at the flat edge. Cut a small pearl from shiny white paper to glue inside.

## How Many Pearls in a Necklace?

Have each child use a string to measure around his neck. Add 2" (5.08 cm) to each. Cut the string that length. Have the children cut small pearls from shiny white shelf paper to glue next to each other all around the necklace. Count the number of pearls it takes to make the necklace.

Line up the number of oysters from the activity above that it takes to make one necklace.

## Babies on Backs

Place some long scarves in the housekeeping center with the babies. Have the children use the scarves to tie the babies to their backs or onto a broom handle (tree limb) like a hammock. (Warn them not to try this with their babies at home!)

## How Far to the Bottom?

Measure six fathoms on your floor or in the gym. Have the children take a deep breath, walk to the other end, stay as long as they can and return to the starting line. Time the children to see how long they can hold their breath at the bottom of the diving pool.

# Canada

McNeer, M., and Ward, L. (1954). *Little Baptiste*. Boston: Houghton Mifflin Company. (Ages 6-9).

The farm that belonged to the Little Baptiste's family seemed to be going downhill. Everyone was too tired to work. Little Baptiste went into the forest to find a way to help. He returned with an elephant, giraffe, and several other animals. Each of the animals worked on the farm, but then started eating the stored goods. Little Baptiste went into the forest to find help. He found the circus band looking for lost circus animals.

## Discussion Questions

1. What responsibilities did the people in Little Baptiste's family have?
2. How do those responsibilities compare to the ones the people in your family have?
3. What type of special work could the circus animals do where you live?

## Classroom Activities

### Circus Animals

Divide the children into teams of three. Give each child a large piece of paper the size you want one of the circus animals. Have him draw the animal with pencil, get it approved by you (for size mostly), outline it in black and paint it in.

Post these on a bulletin board.

### Work for the Animals

Choose one of the animals each day and generate jobs that the animal might do in your classroom, school, community. Have the children illustrate and write about the jobs and post them near the animals.

### Work for the Family

Trace around three children to make pictures of the Little Baptiste's family. Color in each of the people. Label each person. Find in the story what the family members do and list those jobs near each person.

### Work for My Family

On storybook paper have the children draw pictures of the members of their family. Label each member.

Have the children write about what responsibilities members of their families have.

Compare the work of Little Baptiste's family with the work of the children's families. Talk about why there are different types of chores and same types of chores.

# Black American

Mendez, P. (1989). *The Black Snowman.* New York: Scholastic, Inc. (Ages 4-7).

A young boy hates being black, thinking everything that is black is bad. He and his brother build a snowman from the polluted blackened snow and dress it with the magic kente. The black snowman comes to life to show the boys that being alive and feeling good about yourself is what is important.

### Discussion Questions

1. What black things did Jacob think were bad? Are they really bad because they are black?
2. Why was the black snowman a hero?
3. How did the kente help in the story?
4. How can you earn or make money to buy things?

# Classroom Activities

### Reading the Story

In Africa, the kente is wrapped around the storyteller before the stories are told, restoring the stories to the mind of the storyteller. Place a piece of brightly colored African cloth around you before you tell the story.

### A Black Snowman

Give the children a piece of white paper on which to glue a black snowman. Give them several sizes of black squares. Have them cut off the corners to make circles and glue them to their paper. Decorate with eyes, nose, mouth and a brightly colored piece of cloth (kente) around the shoulders.

Children can then be invited to make snowpeople of any color.

by Michaela

### Can Collecting

Jacob and Peewee collect cans to buy a gift for their mother for Christmas. Many times children want to buy gifts for people in their school or for their classroom and do not have the money. Collecting cans throughout the year can help them buy that special gift. Obviously, you must talk about how to collect these cans safely.

### Are They Good or Bad?

Have each child collect three things in the room, each of a different color. Have the child name what he found and determine whether or not it is good or bad, based on its color.

# Navajo

Miles, M. (1971). *Annie and the Old One.* Boston: Little, Brown and Company. (Ages 6-9).

Annie is a young Navajo girl living with her mother, father and grandmother. She and her grandmother share many wonderful times together. As Annie's mother weaves, the Old One tells them that, when the rug is finished, she will return to Mother Earth. Annie does everything she can so that the rug cannot be finished. Eventually the Old One talks with her and tells her she cannot stop time. Annie begins to help with the weaving.

## Discussion Questions

1. What did Annie's grandmother tell her would happen when her mother finished weaving the rug?
2. Annie lived with her mother, father and grandmother. Who lives with you?
3. Annie tried to distract her mother. How do you distract your mother?

## Classroom Activities

### Families

Annie lives with her mother, father and grandmother. Talk with the children about who lives with them. Have each child fold a piece of large paper. At the top of the paper draw and label the members of Annie's family. At the bottom of the paper draw and label the members of your own family.

### Unweaving

Annie tries to unweave the rug her mother is working on in order to make her grandmother live longer. Unweaving is a complicated task. Give each child a small piece of cloth that can be unwoven. Ask him to unweave it and watch what happens as he does.

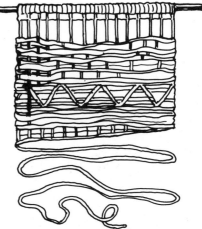

### Weaving

Weaving takes a long time. If you have access to a person who weaves on a large loom, ask him if the children can come to watch as he weaves.

If you want to try weaving in the classroom, try pot holders to begin with. Older children can do finger weaving. Paper woven place mats make nice gifts. Vary the shape and colors of paper to fit the season.

GA1431

# Mexico

Politi, L. (1964). *Lito and the Clown*. New York: Charles Scribner's Sons.

Lito loses his pet kitten Paquita when a stray dog happens by and chases it down the street. Lito goes to find her and sees the clown on stilts from the carnival who is the tallest man in town. He promises to help him find his kitten. Lito goes to the carnival and the stray dog chases the kitten across the stage. Lito gets the kitten and the carnival gets the dog.

## Discussion Questions

1. How did Lito lose his kitten? Whose fault was it?
2. What types of things do you think Lito does to take care of his kitten?
3. When you lose something, how do you go about trying to find it?

# Classroom Activities

### Where's the Cat?

Choose one child to be Lito and one child to be a kitten. Have Lito hide his eyes while the kitten hides. When Lito tries to find the kitten, have the children meow really loud when the dog is close and be quiet when the dog is not close.

### At the Carnival

There were many things at the carnival that came to Lito's town. Reread the story to the children, and when you come to something that was at the carnival have them hold up a construction paper balloon. On one of the balloons, write what it was that was at the carnival.

When you are finished, have the children illustrate on white sheets of paper what it was that they "saw" at the carnival. Post them on a bulletin board. Put the balloons at the top of the bulletin board and connect them to the pictures with string.

# Chinese American

Politi, L. (1960). *Moy Moy*. New York: Charles Scribner's Sons. (Ages 6-9).

Moy Moy and her brothers live in Los Angeles and live above their shop. They get ready to celebrate the Chinese New Year. The story is similar to Politi's *Juanita* which is about a Hispanic child in Los Angeles.

## Discussion Questions

1. What are some of the things that are in Moy Moy's favorite shop?
2. What is Moy Moy's real name? Why do people call her Moy Moy?
3. If you could buy a present for your best friend, what would it be?
4. What made Moy Moy afraid of the lion?

## Classroom Activities

### Chinese Writing

Chinese writing is done with a brush. Give each child a strip of adding machine tape, and place it lengthways on a table. With a watercolor brush, make shapes that look like Chinese writing. They can copy the phrase "Happy New Year, Moy Moy" from the book.

### Colorful Kites

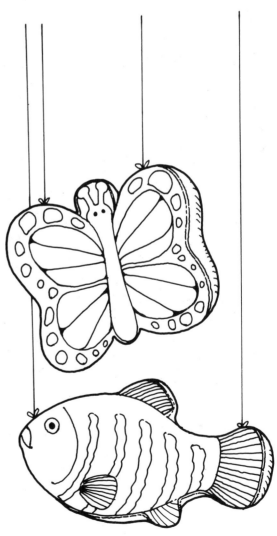

Give each child a large pattern of a butterfly or fish. Have him trace around it twice to make a front and a back for his "kite." Paint the front and the back with bright colors. Let it dry. Staple the edges together except for one. Stuff it with newspaper or tissue. Staple it closed. Hang from the ceiling.

### Lanterns

Fold a piece of construction paper in half lengthways. Use a ruler to mark off 1" (2.54 cm) on the edge that is not folded. Cut from the fold to the line every 1" (2.54 cm). Open it up. Fold to glue the short end to the other short end.

To make a candle for the lantern, paint a toilet paper roll to make the candle. Stuff one end with yellow-red-orange tissue to make the flame.

# Asian American

Politi, L. (1975). *Mr. Fong's Toy Shop.* New York: Charles Schribner's Sons. (Ages 6-9).

Mr. Fong makes toys for the children including juggling sticks, yo-yos, and puppets. Children are in a lantern parade and celebration at the first full moon of mid autumn, the Moon Festival.

## Discussion Questions

1. What was your favorite toy that Mr. Fong made?
2. How do you celebrate a harvest?
3. What crops are grown where you live?
4. What types of things did the children do in this story?

## Classroom Activities

### Juggling

In the story children can see jugglers. Let them try to juggle. Nerf balls are fine. Start with one ball. Toss it up and catch it with one hand. When children are pretty good at this, try tossing the ball up with the other hand and catching it with that hand. Try tossing one ball from one hand to the other. The next step is to toss two balls up at the same time and catch them. Three is for experts only.

### Yo-Yos

Provide the children with some yo-yos to work with in the classroom. Make sure the strings are the right length for them. Yours will need to be longer.

### Shadow Puppets

Provide a shadow puppet stage for the children. Place a lamp on the floor. Near it put up a sheet. Let the children make people, animals, houses, cars and put them on strings attached to sticks.

Hang them over the edge of the sheet and watch the shadows that they make. More advanced children can make up a story to go with the puppets or retell a story that they already know.

### Ribbon Dances

Give each child a long scarf or two long pieces of crepe paper. Show various ways to move the ribbons using large arm motions. Put each in his own space, put on the music, and watch the colors sway with the beat of the music.

GA1431

# Mexico

Politi, L. (1963). *Rosa*. New York: Charles Scribner's Sons.

Rosa lives with her mother, father and brother in Mexico. She rides to school with her brother on a horse, learns to read, write and draw in school. On the way home they go through town where she sees an expensive doll that she wants. Her brother tells her that if she wishes hard enough that her wish might come true. Well, she does get a "doll" to play with, but it comes at Christmas in the form of a baby sister.

## Discussion Questions

1. What did Rosa do in school? What do you do in school?
2. What did Rosa and her brother see on the way to school? What do you see?
3. Did Rosa get her wish? Why or why not?

## Classroom Activities

### Cat and Mouse

Rosa and the children play Cat and Mouse outside at recess. Read the directions carefully to the children and have them play when they get outside.

### Valero

Many times a valero (a wooden ball with a hole in it attached to a string and stick) is available in Hispanic neighborhood markets. Get a couple for your classroom and let the children try to learn the skill. You will find yourself trying, too.

### Rosa's Trip to School, My Trip to School

Give each child a long piece of paper which is folded in half lengthwise. Have the child draw in sequence the things that Rosa sees on her way to school in the top row.

Ask the child to draw in sequence the things that he sees on his way to school in the bottom row.

Compare what the children see and what Rosa sees. Place markers on the things that are the same. When they have finished that task, cut the two rows apart.

Place the children in pairs. Have them compare their ways to school with their partners, placing markers on the things that are the same. Switch partners to find which children have the most things in common. See if they can figure out why.

### Can I Play with Baby?

Rosa is glad to have a baby sister so she can have someone to play with. Obviously, it will be some time until that can be done.

Have each child make a list of things that he likes to play. Go back over the list and place a baby sticker next to each one that a baby can do. (You probably won't need baby stickers.)

# United States/Mountain Life

Rylant, C. (1982). *When I Was Young in the Mountains.* New York: E.P. Dutton. (Ages 4-7).

This story is about the author's memories from her childhood growing up in Appalachia.

## Discussion Questions

1. What kind of work did the grandfather in this story do?
2. What is a johnny-house and where was it located?
3. Tell about some pleasant or special memory of yours.

## Classroom Activities

### Corn Bread

The family in this book ate pinto beans and fried okra with their corn bread. Use a square sheet of yellow or white construction paper as a piece of corn bread. Ask your students to make lists of all the kinds of food that their families like to eat with corn bread.

CORN BREAD 'n'
1. chili and burgers
2. steak and corn
3. hot dogs and chips

### The Swimming Hole

Give each student a sheet of construction paper. Ask him to cut out a hole in the paper and tape a piece of blue cellophane over the hole. This will be the water in the swimming hole. Students are then to draw trees, grass, etc., around the swimming hole. Drawings of people swimming can be colored, cut out, and pasted on the front of the blue cellophane. Other objects like snakes or fish that are under the water can be colored, cut out and pasted to the back of the cellophane to make them look like they are underwater.

### Shelling Beans and Braiding Hair

Grandmother worked with the children shelling beans or braiding hair. Children can shell or snap beans to boil for a snack. Others may practice braiding with thick yarn, jute, or doll's hair.

GA1431

# Puerto Rican Child in United States

Simon, N. (1967). *What Do I Say?* Chicago: Albert Whitman & Company. (Ages 4-7).

The author attempts to identify common activities that all children do and gives them language. The child in the story is a Puerto Rican child in a large American city trying to figure out what it is that he should say for each activity. All children can relate to the language presented. Good morning! All done! Bye-bye. My name is Manuel.

## Discussion Questions

1. What does Manuel do all day?
2. What does Manuel do during the day that you don't do?
3. If you were to make a book about things you do each day, what would you include?

## Classroom Activities

### Same and Different

Young children need to be aware of the similarities and differences in the activities that people do. They can then compare them to the things that they do. Choose some of the topics below and do this activity with the children.

Give each child a piece of paper folded into four squares. Ask him to draw four things related to the topic. Older children can write what they have done, using action words. Younger children can dictate what the pictures show.

When each child is finished, he is to put his name in each box and cut the paper into four pieces along the fold lines.

Graph the results to see how many children do the same and different things.

## What do you do at home?

## What do you do at school?

## Getting ready for school.

## Getting ready for bed.

### Phrase of the Day

Manuel learns to say socially acceptable things in this story. Post one of these each day and encourage the children to use the phrase of the day.

## Thank you.

**Excuse me.**                    **It's my turn.**

**Let's play.**                    **Please help me.**

# Hispanic

Stanek, M. (1989). *I Speak English for My Mom*. Niles, IL: Albert Whitman & Company. (Ages 4-7).

A young girl and her mother move to the United States after the father dies wishing his daughter could grow up and go to college in the United States. The mother speaks no English and Lupe must speak for her. Daily routines that would normally be simple are difficult for one who speaks no English. In order to get a better job, the mother takes classes in English.

## Discussion Questions

1. Why did Lupe and her mother move to the United States?
2. Why was it difficult for her mother in the United States?
3. How might you communicate with someone if you couldn't speak his language?

## Classroom Activities

**Things My Mom Can Do**

Lupe has to do some things for her mom, but her mom can do some things for herself. Have each child fold a piece of paper into four boxes. In each box he is to draw a picture of something that his mom can do. Younger children can dictate to you what the picture is about. Older children can write a sentence telling what his mom is doing. Cut the paper into four boxes. Graph the results and then make a book to take home.

**Things My Mom Cannot Do**

Do the same type of activity as above but change the focus.

**Learning Some Spanish**

The book provides some Spanish words that the children can use throughout the day or week.

Muchas gracias–many thanks. Buenas noches–good night. If you have any Spanish-speaking children in your classroom, solicit help from their parents and make a list of more Spanish words you can learn. For more words, see follow-up activities for *Juanita*.

**What's in the Bag?**

Find a grocery store in your area that handles foods that are packaged elsewhere and do not have the primary language written on them. Buy some with pictures and some without pictures. Put the groceries in a bag. Bring them out one at a time. Have the children try to guess what is in them. For the ones where there is no writing and no clue, have someone who reads the language come in to read to the children.

# Vietnam

Surat, M.M. (1983). *Angel Child, Dragon Child*. New York: Scholastic, Inc. (Ages 6-9).

This fiction story is based on some information given a high school teacher who is a free-lance writer. The young girl and her father and children are able to move here from Vietnam, but there is not enough money for her mother to come. Nguyen Hoa (Ut) goes to school where the children make fun of her. She is lonely and misses her mother. In the end, she tells her story to the school and the children in the school plan a fair to earn money to bring Mother to the United States.

## Discussion Questions

1. Why was Ut unhappy in school?
2. How were the schools in Vietnam different from the schools in the United States?
3. What parts of the story were sad? What parts were happy?
4. If Ut came to your school, how could you make her feel comfortable?

## Classroom Activities

### Mom in a Matchbox

Ut had a picture of her Mother in a matchbox that she kept close at hand. Have each child trace around the bottom of the matchbox and cut out the rectangle. Send home the rectangle with a note to the parents requesting a picture of the parent–mom or dad–that could be cut to that size.

Paint the matchbox. Let it dry. Spray with acrylic to keep the paint from flaking off. Decorate the box. Glue the picture into the bottom of the box.

### Pair Up for Stories

Ut and Raymond are told they must work together to write Ut's story. Raymond writes the story, and Ut draws pictures in the margins.

If your children are writers, pair up the children in your classroom to write a story about their likes. After one story per pair is written, share them with the class. Return to the pairs to switch roles.

If your children are too young, pair them up with older children in the building or in a local school. Let your children tell their partners the stories to write and your children can illustrate the pictures.

### Angel Child, Dragon Child

On separate charts list words or phrases that describe what an Angel Child or a Dragon Child might do. Have each child make a small illustration to place beside each.

# Hispanic

Todd, B. (1972). *Juan Patricio*. New York: G.P. Putnam's Sons. (Ages 4-7).

Juan Patricio wants a job to make money like his two big brothers and his two big sisters. But he could not find a job that fit him until he became a dog sitter for Blancocito.

## Discussion Questions

1. Why did Juan Patricio want a job?
2. What jobs do you think would be just right for Juan Patricio?
3. What jobs do you have?
4. What would be the best way for you to earn money?

## Classroom Activities

Each of the activities listed is one that Juan tried in the story. Ask children whether or not it makes any difference who does the jobs, boys or girls, young or old, etc.

### Making Beds

Young children need to learn to make their beds but that isn't always easy. You can help by having a small bed for them to make. Use a crib mattress and a fitted crib sheet. Cut a top sheet the right size. Use crib blankets, a small pillow and a quilt for a bedspread.

Demonstrate how the bed should be made. Let the children take turns.

### Hanging the Laundry

Put up a clothesline along one wall. Place ten items in a clothes basket for the children to hang up. Have them keep track of how many of the clothes fall onto the floor. Remember to remind them that it is a difficult task and that they will get better at it if they continue to try.

### Painting

Place one large piece of butcher paper on a wall for the children to paint. Place papers on the floor in front of the area. This can later be used as the backdrop for a mural. Give them paint, paintbrushes, and smocks, and let them paint. Have them check each other out at the end of the painting to see how much got on them, how much on the wall, and how much on the papers on the floor.

### Pet Care

Post the care procedures for the class pet in checklist form with pictures beside each chore. Assign different children to do the tasks each day by placing their name cards beside the tasks.

GA1431

# European American

Turner, Ann. (1985). *Dakota Dugout*. New York: Macmillan Publishing Company. (Ages 4-7).

*Dakota Dugout* is an easy-to-read story of a woman describing her experiences living with her husband in a sod house on the Dakota prairie.

### Discussion Questions
1. When the woman first arrived in Dakota and saw the sod house she cried. Why did she cry?
2. Where did the snakes come from that fell on their bed?
3. Why did she take rope with her when she moved to Dakota?

## Classroom Activities

### Moving

The woman packed all she had when Matt sent for her–cups, pots, dresses, and rope. Ask each student to list on a sheet of paper what he would take with him if he moved to a very rural setting. Some of them may have little understanding of a rural setting. You may need to talk about life in the country to help them understand some differences between urban and rural life. Post the lists and summarize what items they are going to take. Discuss what they will use each item for living in the country. Help them to see that some necessary items in one place are not as necessary in another place.

### Talking to the Animals

If they lived on an isolated farm or ranch, how would they spend their day and besides their family who would they talk to and play with? Give each child a 9" x 12" (22.86 x 30.48 cm) sheet of construction paper. Fold the paper in half so that each half is 9" x 6" (22.86 x 15.24 cm). Ask each to draw a picture of a country scene that includes him and some animals that could be his friends in the half on the left. In the other half he should write a description about what is happening in the picture he drew.

On the Farm
When I lived on a farm there were many things I would do. My very favorite thing to do was to walk through the corn fields with my friend Max (my pig). We laugh and talk as we walk through the fields.
Becky G.

### Pack Up to Go

Just what would you take with you if you had to move tomorrow? Give each child a piece of brown construction paper. Write "My Suitcase" at the top. Have each cut out or draw items on white paper to indicate the things he would take with him. Tape a second piece of construction paper over it to make it open/close like a suitcase.

# Black American

Udry, J.M. (1966). *What Mary Jo Shared.* Chicago: Albert Whitman & Company. (Ages 6-9).

Mary Jo couldn't think of a thing to share during sharing time at school. Each day the teacher asked if she was ready and Mary Jo replied, "Not yet." She wanted to share something that no one else had shared. She thought and thought and finally asked her father to go to school with her to hear her share something. Guess what! She shared her father.

## Discussion Questions

1. What were some of the things Mary Jo thought about sharing but did not?
2. How did she feel each day when the teacher asked her if she was ready to share?
3. If you could bring one of your relatives to school to share, what would you say about him/her?

## Classroom Activities

**What Do Parents Do All Day?**

Ask each child to bring one thing from home that tells something about what one of his parents does all day. When he has it at school, ask him to tell about his parent, what he does all day, and how he uses the object that he has brought to remind him about what his parents do all day.

**Parent Day**

Ask parents to come to school for a day to share with the class what they do all day. Schedule only one parent each day. It will take a long time, but it will allow the child to tell about his parent, the children to ask questions, and the parent to embellish whatever is said.

After each parent's visit, have each child draw a picture of one thing that the child's parent does. Put the pictures into a book to send home with the child. Put the title on the book, *What _____ Does All Day.*

**Sharing Time**

At the beginning of the week, send a note home telling the child/parents that the child will be allowed to bring something special from home to share one day that week. Try to schedule five to six per day.

Themes may be used: Colors, Beginning Letter Sounds, Themes, etc.

Other Mary Jo books: *What Mary Jo Wanted* and *Mary Jo's Grandmother*

# Hungary

Varga, J. (1969). *Janko's Wish*. New York: William Morrow & Company. (Ages 6-9).

A delightful tale of lazy Janko who did nothing on his grubby farm until one day when he helped the queen of the gypsies who granted him one wish. He decided to wish for a bag of gold but spent days cleaning up his place, farming his land and working from morning til night to find a place to hide it. In the end he did not wish for gold but for a beautiful wife. His wish was granted.

## Discussion Questions

1. How could you tell that Janko was lazy?
2. Janko thought of many places to hide his gold. Where were some of them, and why did he decide they wouldn't work?
3. Do you think the wish that Janko wished was granted by the queen of the gypsies? Why or why not?
4. If you had one wish, what would you wish for? Why?

## Classroom Activities

### Grubby Farms

Ask the children to draw pictures of farms–not grubby farms. Take the pictures outside and smudge dirt and leaves onto the pictures to make them look grubby. Collect litter from the school yard and glue it onto the pictures where the farmyard is. Post them on a "Janko's Grubby Farm" bulletin board.

### Janko's Housecleaning

Take the day off to do a thorough cleaning of your classroom and chalk it up to role-playing Janko. Assign children to clear the shelves, wash the shelves, replace the items on the shelves, straighten books, wash tables, etc. Use nice smelling cleaners–shaving cream will do–so the whole school will know what you are doing. The children will have great fun, and you will have a wonderfully clean room.

### Hide the Gold

Tie a newspaper into a yellow cloth napkin or handkerchief. Place all the children in the circle and choose one to be Janko. All the children hide their eyes and sing to the tune of "London Bridge":

Janko, go and hide the gold,
Hide the gold, hide the gold.
Janko, go and hide the gold.
Where will he hide it?

**When it is hidden, children find it singing.**

Children, go and find the gold,
Find the gold, find the gold.
Children, go and find the gold.
Where did he hide it?

GA1431

# Native American

White Deer of Autumn. (1983, 1991). *Ceremony in the Circle of Life.* Hillsboro, OR: Beyond Words Publishing, Inc. (Ages 6-9).

White Deer of Autumn presents the four colors of the four directions in a Wheel of Life, a symbol which has universal appeal to Native American people. The care of the earth, of nature's givings is stressed.

## Discussion Questions

1. What does the author present for each of the four colors of the Wheel of Life?
2. What other things do you know that are those colors?
3. How does the Star Spirit tell Little Turtle to take care of the earth?
4. What things do you do to take care of the earth?

# Classroom Activities

### The Four Colors

In the story the Star Spirit shows Little Turtle the Wheel of Life with its four colors and asks him to spin it. In doing so, the four colors become brown, the color of the earth.

Give each child a bit of each of the four colors red, white, black and yellow, a brush and a small piece of white paper. Have him first dab a bit of each color on the paper, one in each corner. In the center, his task is to join the four colors (not from the corners, but from the paint) to make brown. Examine the different shades that he gets.

Take it outside and compare it to the earth in your area. You might be able to remix and get a closer match.

### North, South, East and West

Star Spirit tells Little Turtle of the four directions. Post *N*, *S*, *E* and *W* on the walls of your room to show the children where the directions are when you are in your room. As they leave the room, ask them what direction they are going.

As the children are ready, have them examine maps and locate north, south, east, and west.

### Find the Circles

There are many circular things in nature, in humans, in the environment in general. Go on a circle hunt. Give each child a circle of construction paper and let him go find things outside that are circular or circles. On the circle he can draw what he finds and label it.

GA1431

# Asian American

Yashima, T. (1958). *Umbrella*. New York: Viking Press. (Ages 4-7).

Momo receives an umbrella and a pair of boots for her third birthday. She wants desperately to wear them. She tries to convince her mother she needs them for the sun and for the wind, but her mother insists she wait for rain. When it does rain, she walks to nursery school without holding her mother's hand for the first time.

## Discussion Questions

1. What did Momo get for her birthday?
2. What special things did Momo do on the day that it finally rained?
3. What are some special things that you have for the rain?

## Classroom Activities

### Wash Away Art

Children love to draw on the sidewalk with chalk. It is a good thing to check it out with your administrator first, and try to do it right before a rain. The large sidewalk chalk breaks less easily, but regular chalk will do.

### Dry Away Art

An alternative to the Wash Away Art is to have the children draw on the hot concrete with water and paintbrushes. The more they paint, the more that disappears.

### What Shall I Wear?

Momo waited a long time for just the right weather for her new umbrella and boots. Children can begin to make judgments about the weather and clothing. The beginnings should be taking a look at the weather and determining which of their wraps to wear outside.

From there you can use pictures–matching pictures of weather with clothing from catalogs and clothing for the right weather.

### Drip, Drip, Drop

The rain made an interesting sound on Momo's umbrella. Drip water from the faucet on various things–a tin cup, a lid, a cup of water, etc. After the experimenting, pair the children, let them listen to several sounds and then have one make the sound while the other tries to guess how it is made.

# Native American

Yolen, J., and Moser, B. (1990). *Sky Dogs*. San Diego: Harcourt Brace Jovanovich Publishers. (Ages 6-9).

This story about how the horses came to the Native American people is derived from several of the Blackfeet legends about horses and one about the Blackfeet creator, Old Man.

## Discussion Questions

1. What were some of the ways Blackfeet used animals?
2. Why did the Blackfeet call horses Sky Dogs?
3. Listen to the different names of the people in the story. How do you think they got their names?

## Classroom Activities

### In the Grass Swee-Swash, Swee-Swash

As the people travelled across the grass, their moccasins made sounds in the grass. Have the children go for a walk in some crunchy area and listen to the noises that their shoes make. Have them try to put words to it. Have children draw pictures of their walk and label them "The grass beneath our feet sang _____."

### What's in a Name?

The Blackfeet names are related to what they do. Ask the children in your room to think of names for their friends based on things they know they can do, such as He-Who-Hits-the-Ball-Far, She-Who-Sings-Like-a-Bird, He-Who-Talks-a-Lot.

### Brown and Gold Mural

Give the children different shades of brown, tan, gold and yellow paper. One piece of brown can be the background for the mural on the bulletin board.
Have them draw pictures from the book on the scraps with black pen, cut them out, and glue them onto the background. The development of the mural can take several days.

### Cradleboards

In the story a mother sang a cradleboard song softly to her child. If you have a picture of a cradleboard, show one to the children.
Have the children make a cradleboard for the dolls in the housekeeping area. Use a portion of a cardboard box, a blanket to lay against it, a blanket to wrap around the baby, and something to wrap around the baby to "tie" it to the board.

# Nonfiction

# Eskimo

Alexander, B., and Alexander, C. (1985). *An Eskimo Family*. Minneapolis: Lerner Publications Company. (Ages 6-9).

This book describes the life of a fifteen-year-old Eskimo boy and his family who live in the world's most northern village, Siorapaluk, Greenland.

## Discussion Questions

1. Where does this family get their food? Where do you get yours?
2. Since they don't have running water in the village, how do they get their water in the winter when the sea is frozen?
3. Compare the way your family entertains themselves and how the Eskimos entertain themselves.
4. What are the different responsibilities of each family member in the Eskimo family? In your family?

## Classroom Activities

### Carving

Eskimos often carved figures out of soapstone and ivory. Give each child a bar of soap and a plastic knife. Let him carve a figure from the soap. These figures can be suspended from the ceiling or lights by pushing a thread through the top of the figure using a darning or other large needle. This should be done by you or another adult in the room.

### What Do I Remember?

Give each child a piece of paper and have him fold it so that he has divided the paper into six boxes of equal size. Ask him to think about this story of an Eskimo family and draw one thing in each box that he remembers from the story. When he is finished, the boxes can be cut apart and stapled together to make a book. Let each child tell his story about this family, using the pictures in his book to guide him.

# Hispanic

Brown, T. (1986). *Hello, Amigos!* New York: Henry Holt and Company. (Ages 4-7).

This book chronicles a day in the life of a Mexican American boy who lives in San Francisco. This day is also his birthday.

## Discussion Questions

1. What does Frankie do that shows he is happy?
2. What special things happened to Frankie at school because it was his birthday?
3. How does your family celebrate birthdays?

## Classroom Activities

### Happy Birthday

Ask your students to talk about how their families celebrate birthdays. Lead them to tell how their last birthday was celebrated. Give each child a piece of paper that has been divided into six boxes. Let him draw pictures of presents or activities from his last birthday celebration. These boxes can be cut apart, sequenced in some order and stapled together to make a scrapbook of his last birthday celebration. Give each child a cover sheet for the book and let him design a cover for the book and attach it to the front of the book prior to stapling the pictures together.

### I Have a Corona!

Give each child a 6" x 18" (15.24 x 45.72 cm) sheet of construction paper. Have him cut out some triangles along one of the long sides. See the corona (crown) that Frankie's teacher made him in the book. Let each child decorate the crown by drawing designs on one side of the strip of construction paper with glue and sprinkling glitter over the glue. Set aside to dry.

After the glue has dried, help the child make a circle with the strip of construction paper and after measuring the rounded strip to his head, staple the two ends together. He can wear his corona for the day.

GA1431

# Native American

Chief Seattle (Susan Jeffers). (1991). *Brother Eagle, Sister Sky: A Message from Chief Seattle.* New York: The Dial Books. (Ages 6-9).

This book is a paraphrase of a speech that Chief Seattle gave when he was asked to sell the last of his tribe's land to the white man. He talks of caring for the land, of not owning it, and warns of what will happen if the land is not taken care of. The message is that in our zeal to build and possess, we may lose all that we have.

## Discussion Questions

1. Who do you think Chief Seattle thinks owns the land?
2. What happens if we don't take care of the land? Of our things?
3. How can we take care of the land?

## Classroom Activities

### Web of Life

Chief Seattle says that we do not weave the web of life, but that we are but a part of it. Give each child a piece of black paper and Elmer's glue colored with white paint. If you don't put the white paint in it, it will come out rather clear.

Have the child make a web on the paper. Examine pictures of spiderwebs before you start.

Let the picture dry overnight.

On the next day, have each child draw small pictures on separate pieces of paper, cut them out and glue them onto the web. He can also cut out pictures from magazines. Pictures can be of things that are living–people, plants, animals, etc.

### Take Care of the Trees

Taking care of the land is critical. Taking care of the trees is critical also. Have the children interview their parents to find out what things in their house have a base in wood products and record their responses on a brown sheet of paper shaped like a log. Place them all on a bulletin board of a large tree entitled "Take Care of the Trees."

### Recycle and Reuse

In order to take care of the land, we must use and reuse what we have rather than trashing everything that we use only once. Staple a strap to a paper sack and hang one over the back of each child's chair for a week to collect all the trash that he would otherwise have thrown away. At the end of the week have the children examine the trash and see what they could reuse by rethinking. Bags and bins can be set up for recycling newspaper, aluminum cans, and glass.

# China

Fisher, L.E. (1986). *The Great Wall of China*. New York: Macmillan Publishing Company. (Ages 6-9).

This is the story of the building of the Great Wall of China with a brief history of it. It was begun 2200 years ago to keep out Mongol invaders.

## Discussion Questions

1. Why did the Chinese emperor have the Great Wall built?
2. How many people and how long did it take to build this enormous wall?
3. What do we use to keep strangers from invading our homes and property?

## Classroom Activities

### The Great Wall

Take your class to the sandbox on the playground. Let them construct a wall using wet sand initially. Tell them to build the wall across the sandbox stretching from one side to the next. Give them little direction except to appoint one of them as the leader. Intervene as necessary to point out to them that teamwork and order is necessary if they are going to accomplish their task. Once the wall is completed, ask for suggestions on how to strengthen the wall to keep it from collapsing as the sand dries.

### Chops

Point out the red blocks seen throughout the book. Since ancient times, Chinese artists, have stamped their chops–their names and signs–on their work. Give each child a potato half and a plastic knife. Show him how to carve away the potato leaving the letters of his initials. Once his stamp is finished, let him press the potato stamp onto an ink pad and stamp his chop (name) on a piece of paper. During that day let him put his chop on any papers instead of writing his name.

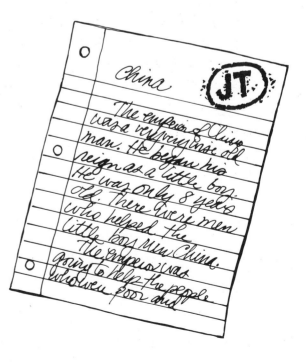

# Africa

Haskins, J. (1989). *Count Your Way Through Africa*. Minneapolis: Carolrhoda Books, Inc. (Ages 6-9).

The numbers one through ten in Swahili (with phonetic spellings) are presented with each number introducing a concept about Africa and its culture.

## Discussion Questions

1. How do some of the people identify themselves as members of a family?
2. What is special about the stones in Africa?
3. What types of animals could you see in Africa? Do you see those where you live?
4. People use a kumi to do their hair. What does it remind you of that you have seen or used?

## Classroom Activities

### Where Is Africa?

Show the children a map or globe, locating where they live and where Africa is. Note what is in between the countries, their distance from the equator, their placement in the northern or southern hemisphere.

### Nine-Line Poems

The warriors made up a poem which had nine lines. Ask the children to write about what they have learned from this book in nine lines. (For younger children, fold a piece of paper into nine rows and have them draw something on each line.)

### Animals Native to Africa

Let the children draw animals that are native to Africa. Use material swatches to make stripes or dots. Cut them out.

On a separate sheet of paper, paint a picture of the environment where each animal lives, including trees, deserts, rocks, ponds, etc. This could be a class project and would then become a larger mural.

When the painting is dry, glue the animals in place.

# Mexico

Haskins, J. (1989). *Count Your Way Through Mexico*. Minneapolis: Carolrhoda Books, Inc. (Ages 6-9).

The numbers one through ten in Spanish (with phonetic spellings) are presented with each number introducing a concept about Mexico and its culture.

## Discussion Questions

1. The heritage and culture of Mexico comes from what two peoples?
2. Name some arts and crafts for which Mexico is famous.
3. What are some of the foods of Mexico that you have eaten?

## Classroom Activities

### Counting to Ten

Give each student a piece of paper and let him count to ten in Spanish. Then he should write the numbers on a sheet of paper going down the left side and draw one of the Mexican foods or arts and crafts ideas after each number. These can be displayed in the classroom and later taken home.

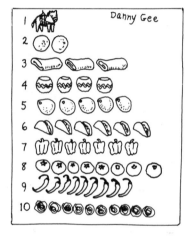

### A Mexican Banquet

The people who have inhabited Mexico have given the world eight foods–corn, chocolate, tomatoes, vanilla, pumpkins, avocados, chilis, and coconuts. Corn is the basic food of the Mexican diet. Tortillas (thin cornmeal pancakes) are served with most meals. Tacos, enchiladas, tamales, quesadillas, chalupas, gorditas, flautas, and tostadas all use tortillas as part of the dish. Provide these foods fixed in traditional Mexican dishes for a classroom banquet.

Depending on the ages of the children in your classroom, let them help prepare as many of these dishes as safety permits.

# Pueblo

Hoyt-Goldsmith, D. (1991). *Pueblo Storyteller*. New York: Holiday House. (Ages 6-9).

Present-day life is explained by April who is ten years old. The history of the Pueblo, traditions, family structure, jobs, education, foods, pottery making, dances, and storytelling are examined with current photographs to show the places, products, and processes. The book concludes with the Pueblo legend, How the People Came to Earth. April is shown both in her Pueblo dress and in contemporary dress.

## Discussion Questions

1. How do April and her grandmother make the bread?
2. What do April and her grandparents do together that you and your grandparents do together?
3. What does April do that you do? What does she do that you don't do?

## Classroom Activities

### Storytellers

As you read this story to the children, ask them to take a good look at how they are sitting, how they are listening and how you are when you read. Compare these things with the storyteller that is made in the story.

### Clay Storytellers

As the teacher, mold a person as a storyteller. Use play dough as a starter. Potter's clay can be used if you know how to use it. Ask each of the children to mold a small person to attach to the storyteller. Place the storyteller in the reading area.

### Play Clothes and Special Clothes

In the story April is shown dressed in various types of clothing. Go through each picture and ask what types of activities April might do dressed as she is. Have children tell you about clothing they have for different activities.

Provide catalogs of children's clothing for children to cut out various types of clothing. When they have piles and piles of pictures, have them sort them into types of activities that can be done in those clothes. Use the sorting for a bulletin board, or let each child glue a couple of pictures to a sheet of paper divided into boxes for each activity.

*Totem Pole* (1989) is a second book by this author which describes the present-day life of David and his father as they choose a tree, cut it down, carve a totem pole, raise it and celebrate its raising.

# Chinese American

Waters, K., and Slovenz-Low, M. (1990). *Lion Dancer: Ernie Wan's Chinese New Year.* New York: Scholastic, Inc. (Ages 4-7).

A true account of one Chinese American family and the preparations they make to celebrate the New Year in Chinatown. It also details the home and work life of this family. Ernie is to perform his first Lion Dance on the streets of New York City.

## Discussion Questions

1. Ernie goes to a special school on Saturdays to learn how to read and write Chinese. What do you learn to do outside of school?
2. Have you eaten Chinese food? What kind of Chinese food have you eaten, and what are your favorite dishes?
3. The Wan family has many traditions for the New Year's holiday? What traditions does your family have for holidays like Christmas, New Year's, Easter, 4th of July, etc.?

## Classroom Activities

### On the Way Home from School

The children walk home from school. There are pictures to show what they see on the way. List all the things these children see on the way home from school. Take a count to see how many of your children see the same things.

Two other books that talk about what children see on the way home are *Our Home Is the Sea* and *Plenty to Watch*.

### Rice, Rice Bowls and Chopsticks

Rice is a staple food for this family. The young child is pictured eating rice with chopsticks.

Give your children a bowl of rice and some chopsticks. Look at the picture to see how the young child holds the chopsticks. Have the rice for a snack–what they can get of it on their chopsticks.

### Drums

The children play dance music on their drums. They also ride on a drum cart at the end of the Lion Dance celebration. Check the other stories in this book about drums in other cultures. See *Jambo Means Hello, Dancing Drum, At the Crossroads, Pueblo Storyteller, The Calypso Alphabet.*

### The Year of the Rabbit

There is a Chinese horoscope at the end of the book. Let the children find out when they and members of their families were born and what "signs" they were born under.

# Biographies

Sitting Bull

Cesar Chavez

Martin Luther King, Jr.

George Bush

Benjamin Franklin

Mahatma Gandhi

Harriet Tubman

# European American

Adler, D.A. (1990). *A Picture Book of Benjamin Franklin.* New York: Holiday House. (Ages 4-7).

Adler presents an informative and picturesque history of the life of Benjamin Franklin, well written for young children. He presents information about when Ben was a child, about his family, about things he liked and didn't like, how he grew up, and what the important events were in his life. The book provides a springboard for many activities.

## Discussion Questions

1. What did Ben like to do as a young child? When he got older?
2. How many children were in Ben's family when he was a child? When he got married?
3. What were some of the things Ben did when he was young that you like to do?
4. What do you think you want to do when you grow up?

# Classroom Activities

**Where Is Boston?**

Locate Boston on a United States map. Place a map pin on the map to show Ben's home. Where do you live? Place a second map pin on the map to show where you live. Are you far or near?

**How Many in Your Family?**

Make a class graph with the boxes at least 6" x 6" (15.24 x 15.24 cm), 15 to 20 boxes long, 15 to 20 boxes high. Give each child a piece of paper smaller than the box. Have him write his name on it.

At circle time, ask how many children are in each child's family and place his name on the graph showing how many children in his family. Place Ben's name on the graph at 17. Discuss how many that might really be and how it would be to live in a family of 17.

**My Best Subjects, My Worst Subjects**

The author tells us about what Ben did well in school and what he did not do well. This happens to us all.

Have the children generate a list of all the types of things that they do in school. Post these on chart paper. Give each child two skin-toned circles. On one have him draw a happy face. On the other have him draw a sad face or straight face. As you read the various things on the chart, have the children place their faces beside the things they do best and the things they do worst. Place Ben's happy face near the handwriting or reading and his sad face near the math.

# Black American

Adler, D.A. (1989). *A Picture Book of Martin Luther King, Jr.* New York: Holiday House. (Ages 4-7).

This simple story about Martin Luther King tells about his life as a child growing up in his family, about his parents, about going to school, about deciding what he wanted to be when he grew up, about the protests, and eventually his assassination.

## Discussion Questions

1. Who was in Martin Luther King's family? Is his family smaller or larger than yours?
2. What did Martin's mom do? His dad? What does your mom do? Your dad?
3. What was Martin's goal in life? What was his dream?
4. What things do you argue about? What are some better ways of solving the problems?

## Classroom Activities

### Moms at Work

Many children today have moms who work outside of the home. Others work in the home. Have children make a book of what moms do when they work. (If you would rather, do the dad's activity listed below for the moms.)

### Dads at Work

Many of the children today have dads who work outside of the home. The others may have dads who work in the home. Ask children to interview their dads about what they do at work. Have each child bring one thing to school to tell about what his dad does at work. After a sharing at circle time, have the children draw a picture of the thing that he brought and post on a bulletin board. (If you would rather, do the mom's activity listed above for the dads.)

### Martin Luther King's Dream of Peace

Dr. King wanted peace in the world. Children would like peace in theirs also. On a cloud-shaped piece of paper write "I Have a Dream." Let the children draw pictures of how they can work and play peacefully with each other, with members of their families, in their neighborhoods, in their communities. Older children can write about what they have drawn on the backs of their pictures. Younger ones can dictate sentences about their pictures. Hang the pictures they make from the ceiling.

GA1431

# India

Bains, R. (1990). *Gandhi: Peaceful Warrior*. Mahwah, N.J.: Troll Associates. (Ages 6-9).

This is the story of the Indian leader whose nonviolent passive resistance tactics influenced reformers in other countries.

### Discussion Questions

1. What was unusual about the "dust school" Mohan Gandhi attended from 5-7?
2. How did the British rulers treat the Indians?
3. Have you ever been treated poorly by someone? How did this make you feel?

## Classroom Activities

### The "Dust School"

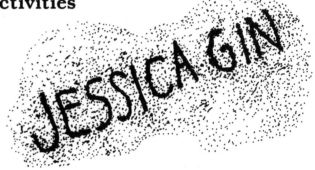

Mohan's teacher, when he was young, drew letters and numbers in the sand floor of the schoolroom because there were no chalkboards, chalk, paper, or ink in the school. The children copied the teacher, each one practicing writing with a stick in the sand.

Take your class out to the playground's sandbox to do your next lesson. Let the children do their writing in the sand instead of using paper and pencil.

### Gullidanda

This is an Indian game played by hitting a wooden peg with a stick. It is a street version of field hockey. Instead of using sticks, let children play a modified form of this game by kicking a wooden peg with their feet and trying to get the peg across a goal. Set the field up similar to field hockey or soccer. Let the children help develop the rules of the game.

### A Beacon for Others

Give every child a piece of paper and ask him to fold it into quarters. In the center of the paper that has been opened flat, each child should write the word *Gandhi*. Then in each quarter, beginning with the quarter in the upper left corner, have the child draw a picture that depicts an event in his life.

GA1431

# Black American

Bains, R. *Harriet Tubman: The Road to Freedom*. U.S.A.: Troll Associates. (Ages 6-9).

Harriet Tubman was born into a slave family and worked hard from the time she was very little. This story presents a realistic picture to young children in terms that they can understand about Harriet's desire for freedom, her trip to freedom, and her helping others.

## Discussion Questions

1. What were slaves allowed to do? What were things they couldn't do?
2. What were some of Harriet's responsibilities when she was a child? What are some of your responsibilities as a child?
3. What did Harriet do to help other people? What things do you do to help others?

## Classroom Activities

### Helping Hands

Place several large hands of various colors on the bulletin board. Have each child trace around his hands at least five times and cut them out. Each time a child does something to help another person, the helped child is to take one of the helper's hands to the teacher who writes on the hand what he did to help and posts it on the bulletin board.

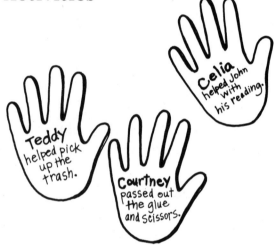

### Bring Smiles to Their Faces

Harriet helped old people. Young children can help them, too, by just bringing smiles to their faces. Ask a nursing home or senior center near your school if your children can provide paintings and other decorations for the people living in the center. If the center is close, have the children walk over to take the gifts to the people themselves and sing a few songs for them while they are there. Be sure to talk about how good it feels to see the smiles on others' faces.

### Train Words

In order to better understand the vocabulary in the story, have the children build a village with a train running through it. Label each part and person—station, stationmaster, depot, conductor, passengers, parcels.

# European American

Behrens, J. (1989). *George Bush: Forty-First President of the United States.* Chicago: Children's Press. (Ages 6-9).

Behrens reviews the life of George Bush, looking at his life as a child, an adolescent, a Navy man, getting married, going to college, raising a family, and going to work. These activities are some that all people do; however, George ended up as President of the United States. Photos help to tell the story.

## Discussion Questions

1. Who was in George Bush's family when he was a child? How was his family like yours? How was it different from yours?
2. What did George like to do when he was younger? What do you like to do?
3. When George got married, he and his wife Barbara had six children, four boys and two girls. One of the girls, Robin, died when she was young. How many children were there in George's family then? How does that compare with your family?

## Classroom Activities

### Where Does George Bush Live?

George was born in Massachusetts, grew up in Connecticut, and went to live in Texas after he graduated from college. He lived in the White House in Washington, D.C., as President of the United States.

On a map, note each place that George Bush lived. How far is each from you? How close?

### What Does a President Do All Day?

What do your children think a President does all day? On a sheet of paper, have each draw a President of the United States. Beside the picture, have him draw some of the things that he thinks the President does. Ask him to write or dictate to you what the President does. Post or send them directly to the President.

### How to Become President

Give each child a piece of long paper. Have him draw pictures to show how he, as a child, should start out, study, and work to become President. Start at the far left side of the strip of paper. After each picture, have him draw a line and number the next picture consecutively. Post them on a bulletin board. Enlarge title below for your display.

GA1431

# European American

Behrens, J. (1988). *Juliette Low: Founder of the Girl Scouts of America*. Chicago: Children's Press. (Ages 6-9).

Behrens reviews the life of Juliette Low, looking at her life as a child, all the interesting things she did throughout her life, her deafness, her joys and her sorrows. She shows how Juliette founded the Girl Guides in Europe and the Girl Scouts in the United States. Photos help to tell the story.

## Discussion Questions

1. Who was in Juliette's family when she was a child? How was her family like yours? How was it different from yours?
2. Juliette did many exciting things throughout her life. Name a few.
3. Juliette could not hear out of one ear and had a hard time hearing out of the other? How did her deafness happen, and how did she deal with it?
4. Why do you suppose really young Girl Scouts are called Daisies? Why do you think Juliette was called Daisy?

## Classroom Activities

### Where Did Juliette Low Live?

Juliette Low was born in Savanna, Georgia, went away to boarding school in New York, got married in Savanna and went to live some time in England.
On a map, note each place that she lived. How far is it from you? How close?

### Things I Do Well, Things I Don't Do Well

The story tells about some of the things that Juliette Low did well in school and some of the things that she did poorly.

Give each child two sheets of paper, four boxes on each, and the name of a subject or activity that you do in school in each box (reading, writing, math, science, spelling, coloring, swinging, riding tricycles, playing basketball, etc.). In each box have the child draw a picture to show what that activity entails.

Cut up the sheets. Have the child put the things he does well in one pile and the things he doesn't do as well in another pile. Staple them together into two books. Make covers for them. Let the children share them with each other, making encouraging remarks.

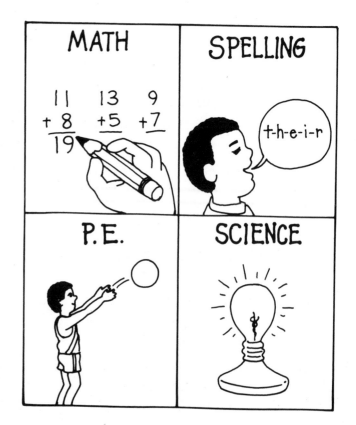

GA1431

# Vietnamese American

Brown, T. (1991). *Lee Ann: The Story of a Vietnamese-American*. New York: G. P. Putnam's Sons. (Ages 6-9).

A young Vietnamese-American girl describes the circumstances that led to her family immigrating to the United States, her family and school life (an ESL class), Saturday activities, and the celebration of TET, the Vietnamese New Year.

## Discussion Questions

1. What is a refugee? How is a refugee different from an immigrant?
2. Why is the Vietnamese New Year similar to the Chinese New Year?
3. Lee Ann is happy about her present. Why are you happy about your present?

## Classroom Activities

### Learning a Language

Students whose first language is not English usually go to a special class (ESL) to learn English. If you have a student in your class whose first langauge is something other than English, have him teach the rest of the class some words and phrases from his native language.

### Hot Dogs

Lee Ann loves hot dogs. Give each student three sheets of 3" x 5" (7.62 x 12.70 cm) pieces of paper and ask him to list a favorite food on each sheet of paper. Choose some helpers to collect the sheets by asking students to hold up their hand if they have written a food you call out on their papers. Once all the sheets of paper have been collected and grouped together, have some helpers count how many listed each different kind of food. Then graph the different kinds of favorite foods named by your students.

### In School

Lee Ann talks about opening the day with the Pledge of Allegiance to the flag. Examine all the other things that she says she does in school. Put check marks beside the ones that your children do each day also.

# Sioux

Fleisher, J. (1979). *Sitting Bull: Warrior of the Sioux*. Mahwah, N.J.: Troll Associates. (Ages 6-9).

This book tells the story of Sitting Bull's life from the time when he was a boy, named Slow, until his death.

## Discussion Questions

1. Why was Slow's name changed to Sitting Bull?
2. Why were the Sioux hunting lands in the Black Hills invaded by white men?
3. Sitting Bull dreamed of a great victory over the Bluecoat soldiers. What victory did he dream of?

## Classroom Activities

### The Growing of a Mighty Chief

Give each child a 6' x 18" (1.82 m x 45.72 cm) piece of construction paper and crayons or markers. Lead your children in a discussion in which you identify the major events in Sitting Bull's life. Write these in chronological order on the chalkboard from left to right. Ask each child to draw a time line of Sitting Bull's life. Using words and pictures, each child should include some of the events listed on the chalkboard on his time line.

### Your Own Time Line

Give each child a 6' x 18" (1.82 m x 45.72 cm) piece of construction paper and crayons or markers. On another sheet of paper have him list some major events in his own life. He should include events like his birth, first tooth, first step, starting school, moving, etc. Now he can select some of the events from his own life and, using words and pictures, make a time line of his own life. These can be sent home as gifts to their parent(s).

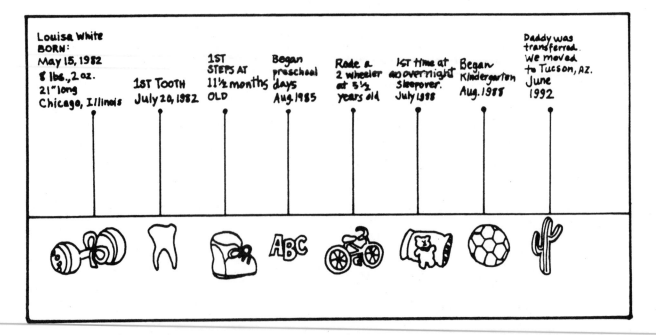

# Hispanic

Franchere, R. (1970). *Cesar Chavez*. New York: Harper & Row Publishers. (Ages 4-7).

This is the story of Cesar Chavez, the leader of the National Farm Workers Association.

## Discussion Questions

1. Tell about Cesar's life growing up in Arizona and California?
2. Why were migrant farm workers cheated and paid low wages?
3. Why are some people treated poorly by others?

## Classroom Activities

### Where in the World Is Cesar Chavez?

Give each child a piece of paper and have him fold it in quarters. In the center of the paper have him write "Cesar Chavez," so that it touches all four quarters. Ask your children to draw a picture of Cesar Chavez as a boy in the upper left quarter. In the quarter below this picture they should draw a map of the southwestern United States and label Yuma, Arizona, the place where Cesar lived until he was ten years old. In the upper right quarter, the children can draw a picture of Cesar during his adult life. Below this quarter, they can draw a map of California and label the cities where Cesar lived and worked.

### What's Valuable?

Cesar and his brother saved tinfoil from various sources to get enough money to buy tennis shoes and shirts. Discuss some classroom needs and how much money would be needed to meet those needs. Ask your children what they could save to sell in order to get the money to buy those things the class needs. Aluminum cans, glass bottles, newspapers, etc., may be suggested.

As a class, decide on one or two of the needs and how you will raise the money to meet these needs. Start the project. Let your children draw posters and write letters to friends, neighbors, and relatives letting them know what the class project is and how they can help. Send the posters home and mail the letters if the children cannot deliver them.

GA1431

# India

Greene, C. (1983). *Mother Teresa: Friend of the Friendless*. Chicago: Children's Press. (Ages 6-9).

The story of Mother Teresa tells about her childhood and her decision to go to India. It tells of the many projects she is involved in with the Missionaries of Charity.

## Discussion Questions

1. How did Mother Teresa decide to help the people in India?
2. Where is India? Is it close to you or far from you?
3. What types of things does Mother Teresa do to help the poor?
4. What types of things can you do to help the poor?
5. If you sent Mother Teresa money, what do you think she would do with it?

## Classroom Activities

### Red Cross Boxes

In times of disaster, the Red Cross sends in personal hygiene boxes which contain combs, toothpaste, toothbrushes, etc. If you get in contact with your local office, they will provide you with information about how to make these boxes and where they might be sent. Our children have filled them for the earthquake victims in Russia and for the tornado victims in Wichita, Kansas.

### Visits for the Old

Mother Teresa talks about going to visit the old people that no one else seems to care about. Ask the local retirement communities and nursing homes if your class can come to visit the people to cheer them up. Take paintings for the walls, learn songs the people might like–the oldies but goodies–and teach the children to shake hands nicely with the people they meet.

### Soup for the Soup Kitchen

In one of the activities listed for *Stone Soup*, it is suggested that you make bone soup. If you have a large pot, take a pot of soup to a local soup kitchen for the poor in your area. This type of project can be undertaken on a monthly basis. It's great for assembly line productions in the classroom (cooperative learning) and great for the giving spirit we need to develop in young children.

# Native American

Greene, C. (1988). *Pocahontas: Daughter of a Chief*. Chicago: Children's Press. (Ages 6-9).

The story of Pocahontas shows the relationship between some of the colonists and some of the Native Americans. Pocahontas was very curious about these new people and the strange things they did, much different than what her family had done for years. She met the new people and became friends with them, saving John Smith from death. People lied to her, telling her John was dead. Eventually she married John Rolfe, went to England as an Indian princess, met with the King and Queen, got sick and eventually died in England.

## Discussion Questions

1. How did Pocahontas help the settlers?
2. How did her father feel about her helping the settlers?
3. Why do you think Pocahontas saved John Smith?
4. Where did Pocahontas go with John Rolfe? What happened there?

# Classroom Activities

### Helping Others

Pocahontas wanted to help others. She did.

Give the children pieces of paper and have them fold them in half. On one side, have them list/draw ways Pocahontas helped others. On the other side list/draw ways they help others. Are any the same? Why or why not?

### Corn on the Cob

One of the most relevant crops of the early days was corn. Plan some activities around corn.

Not only can children eat corn on the cob, they can learn about the makeup of corn by "making" ears themselves. Give each child a toilet paper roll, dried corn (unpopped popcorn will do), strips of green construction or tissue paper. Glue the corn onto the paper roll. Glue several strips of green paper together to make a sleeve for the corn on the cob.

### How Much Will It Make?

Measure $1/4$ c. (60 ml) of unpopped corn. Place bowls of various sizes on a table. Give each child a piece of paper shaped like a popped piece of corn and ask him to place it in the bowl that he thinks will hold the popped corn.

Pop the corn. Pour it into the largest bowl first. "No, that one is too big." When you get to one that is just right–"Yes, that one is just right." Compare the quarter cup of unpopped corn to the bowl of corn.

GA1431

# Hawaii

Hoyt, H.P. (1974). *The Princess Kaiulani*. Honolulu: Island Heritage Books. (Ages 6-9).

A grandmother tells her young granddaughter the story of Princess Kaiulani after she has sent her a doll of the princess. The princess was the last of the royalty in Hawaii and had a short, sad life.

## Discussion Questions

1. How did Victoria become a princess? How was it that she was to become queen?
2. What types of things did she like to do when she was young?
3. Who was in Victoria's family? What types of things did she do with her family?

## Classroom Activities

### Childhood Fun

Ask each of the children to make a list of things he likes to do to have fun at home. Graph the results to see how many of the children like to do each thing. Reread the story of Princess Kaiulani, looking specifically for things she liked to do when she was young. Make a list of these.

Place the things that the Princess liked to do on the graph using gold to denote the royalty.

Compare and contrast the things presented by your children and the Princess. Talk about why the two things are similar or different.

### Princess Kaiulani

Ask each child to draw a portrait of Princess Kaiulani. Look carefully at the pictures of her in the book.

To frame the picture, cut an oval out of a piece of gold paper and put the open piece of gold paper over the portrait that the child has drawn. Post pictures in the room.

### Victoria's Family

Ask the children to draw pictures of the members of Victoria's family–many will include the nurse, some will not.

Compare the pictures with the family structures of the children in your room. Graph the different family structures to show the various types of families.

Make a list of the things that Victoria's parents did–their jobs, responsibilities, etc.

# Black American

Rosenthal, B. (1986). *Lynette Woodard, the First Female Globetrotter.* Chicago: Children's Press. (Ages 6-9).

Lynette grew up in Wichita, Kansas, attended the University of Kansas, played in the World University Games and the Pan American Games, was chosen for the 1980's Olympic team and the 1984 team that won the Olympics, and eventually became the first woman to play for the Globetrotters. The story appears with black and white photos of Lynette in the various stages of her career.

## Discussion Questions

1. How far is Wichita, Kansas, from where you live?
2. How did Lynette get to play for the Globetrotters?
3. What do you want to do when you grow up?

# Classroom Activities

### Where Is Wichita, Kansas?

Locate Wichita, Kansas, on a map. Place a map pin on the map to locate the city. Locate where you live. Place a second map pin on the map. How close are you? How far are you? What else is close to Wichita, Kansas?

### I Can Play Basketball

Basketball is a game of several different skills including dribbling, running and dribbling, making baskets. Try some of these ball skills with your children. Some two-year-olds are amazing dribblers. Some eight-year-olds have a difficult time.

Place a large ball, a smaller ball and some "baskets" in a center for children to play with during free play. Have them try dribbling, walking while dribbling, and making baskets from various marked spots on the floor. More advanced children can keep score.

### When I Grow Up

Just what do you want to be when you grow up? Interview the children one at a time to see what it is that each says he wants to be when he grows up. Write that "occupation" at the top of a piece of paper. (We use that term loosely. They might one day want to be a doctor, the next day a clown and finally one day announce that they want to be a genius when they grow up.)

For an activity, give each child his piece of paper and have him write/draw about what he thinks he will have to do when he grows up as this person.

GA1431

# Chinese American

Say, A. (1990). *El Chino.* Boston: Houghton Mifflin Company. (Ages 6-9).

This is the true story of Bong Way "Billy" Wong, the first Chinese bullfighter in Spain. Billy was the son of Chinese immigrants who grew up in Arizona and was often told by his father, "In America, you can be anything you want to be."

## Discussion Questions

1. What was the first thing Billy wanted to do after high school and why couldn't he do that?
2. Why was he able to be a matador? What abilities did he have?
3. What do you want to be when you grow up, and why do you think you will be successful?

## Classroom Activities

### What Shall I Do When I Grow Up?

As with most of the biographies, ask each of the children to tell you what he wants to be when he grows up. Record these responses on a class chart. Do the following activity, having each child interview his parents about their occupations. Compare the child's responses to his parents'.

### Occupations

Give each child a piece of paper and as a class write down a list of questions they can ask their family members about how they decided on their occupations. These questions should include (1) how old were they when they decided what they wanted to be, (2) what did they want to be and why didn't they or couldn't they become that, (3) do they like what they are now doing and why or why not, (4) if they could do something different, what would they choose and why. Add other questions and send these home for the children to interview their family members.

When the interviews are returned, graph the careers family members of the children identified as children themselves and the careers/occupations they are now in. Talk about the reasons people choose careers/occupations and some of the reasons they change their minds and become or do something different.

GA1431

# Comanche

Verheyden-Hilliard, M.E. (1985). *Engineer from the Comanche Nation: Nancy Wallace*. Bethesda, MD: The Equity Institute. (Ages 6-9).

Nancy Wallace was raised in Faxon, Oklahoma. Her father was from the Comanche Nation, her mother from the Creek Nation. Her favorite subject in school was math, but she did not know what she could do with her skills. A counselor gave her a book, *Women in Engineering,* which she read. She went to the University of Oklahoma to study, got married, had a child and decided school was too hard. A professor got her a summer job working with engineers. She returned to school, graduated and is now an engineer.

## Discussion Questions

1. What did Nancy like about school? What do you like best?
2. What did she like to do in her spare time? What do you do in your spare time?
3. What type of summer reading program did Nancy participate in? What type of summer reading program do you participate in?
4. What were the hard parts of Nancy's life? What were the good parts?

## Classroom Activities

**Where Is Faxon?**

Locate Faxon, Oklahoma, on a United States map. Place a map pin on the map to show Nancy's home. Where do you live? Place a second map pin on the map to show where you live. Are you far or near?

**How Many in Your Family?**

Make a class graph with boxes at least 6" x 6" (15.24 x 15.24 cm), 15 to 20 boxes long, 15 to 20 boxes high. Give each child a piece of paper smaller than the box and write their name on it.

At circle time, ask how many children are in each child's family and place his name on the graph showing how many children in his family. Remember that Benjamin Franklin had seventeen children in his family. How many did Nancy have? Is there anyone in the class with the same family structure?

**I Love Math**

Nancy loved math. At the top of a piece of paper have the child write "I Love Math." On the rest of the sheet, have him write/draw what he knows about math.

**Comanche and Creek**

Find out whatever you can about the Comanche and Creek tribes. Use the information provided in the resources listed at the end of this book.

# Poetry

GA1431

# Africa

Brown, M. (1982). *Shadow*. New York: Aladdin Books, Macmillan Publishing Company. (Ages 4-7).

*Shadow* is a translation from the French poet Blaise Cendrars who portrayed a dancing image–shadow. This translation tells all about shadows, their need for light, where you find them, and superstitions about them.

## Discussion Questions

1. Who/What has a shadow in this story?
2. Who/What do you know that has a shadow?
3. What color are shadows? Why do you think they are always that color?
4. Why do you think the shadow would look like it was dancing in the fire-light?

## Classroom Activities

### Where Is My Shadow?

Take the children outside on a sunny day and have them look at their shadows. Young children may actually be afraid of them, so be aware of how they respond.

Try running from your shadow, stepping on it, jumping over it, and leaving it outside. As children try these things, be sure to ask questions about why they can or cannot do what they are trying to do.

When the children get back into the building, have them again look for their shadows. Sometimes they will see them; sometimes they won't. Try to figure out why.

### Shadow Drawings

After students return to the classroom, have each make a picture with a shadow. First have them draw pictures of themselves, cut them out and trace around them on pieces of black paper. Glue the person onto a piece of blue paper and attach the shadow to the picture. A nice big sun in the corner opposite the shadow will give a nice reason to have a shadow.

### Hand Shadows

On a sunny day or with a large spotlight, provide a blank wall or piece of cardboard for the children to cast hand shadows on. Two straight fingers make great rabbit ears. Two bent fingers make fox ears.

### Measuring Shadows

Place an object outside in the sun where the children can see it periodically during the day. Watch what the shadow does. Trace it; measure it; examine it. Try it again the next day at about the same time. What has happened?

# European American

Fleischman, P. (1988). *Joyful Noise*. New York: Harper & Row Publishers. (Ages 6-9).

The author presents poems to be read by two people simultaneously. All poems are about insects and serve as a fascinating guide to insect facts. The poems could be read by advanced second graders, or the older children in the building could come to read them to your children (Newbery Book).

### Discussion Questions
1. When two people read the poems, how did it make you feel?
2. What interesting things did you hear about (name an insect)?
3. What different words does the author use to tell you that a grasshopper "jumps," a mayfly "flies," a honeybee "works"?
4. What happened to the chrysalis?

## Classroom Activities

### Insect Facts
Divide your classroom into groups. Assign each group one of the poems. Their assignment is to listen to the poem (taped or read to them again) and record the facts they learn about their insect. It will take several readings of the poem. After each reading, a finder can tell about the fact, a recorder can write down the fact, a drawer can illustrate the fact.

### Spinning! Swerving!
How many ways can you say *spinning*? Many of these poems tell about movements using many movement words. A real challenge to young children!

Start with a simple movement like "go." How many ways can you think of to "go" someplace? This is what these insects are doing, going somewhere their way. What are your ways to go someplace?

After they have thought of several, give each child a piece of paper folded into four boxes. Have him illustrate a way to "go" in each box. Write the word in the box.

Cut the boxes out. Put a name on each box. Get back with the group to see how many ways the children came up with, laying like ones in columns to make a graph.

When the graph is finished, allow the children to reclaim their ways to go, make more if they wish, and staple into books.

# Black American

Fufuka, K. (1975). *My Daddy Is a Cool Dude*. New York: The Dial Press. (Ages 6-9).

This collection of poetry reflects life in an urban black community. Most of the poems are about friends, relatives (mama, daddy, brothers, sisters, babies) and others in the community.

### Discussion Questions

Each poem offers insight into a person or an experience. Children can be asked general questions, such as

1. Do you know someone like this? What does he do? How do you know him?
2. Have you ever done something new and exciting and told someone about it? What was it and what did you tell the person about it?

## Classroom Activities

### Pretty Brown Baby

One of the poems presented is "Pretty Brown Baby." It is four lines long. Children can change the word *Brown* to anything they want and chant the poem in a new way. *Brown* can be changed to a different color or words such as *little*, *round*, *fancy*, etc.

Have children bring in baby pictures and let the other childen choose a word to fit the picture describing each child as a baby.

### Big Mama

Another of the poems is about a grandmother who lives down south. Children can fit their own grandmothers into the words of the poem. Each will need his grandmother's name, where she lives, what he eats that is special at her house, a description of her house and the animals that she has.

A note home to parents will get the necessary information.

### What Will a Nickel Buy?

In one of the poems, a child has a nickel to spend and wants to buy something that he can share with his friend.

Survey the children to see what they think a nickel will buy. Put their responses on a round silver piece of paper and post on a bulletin board made like a large nickel. Post the poem at the top.

GA1431

# Caribbean

Joseph, L. (1990). *Coconut Kind of Day: Island Poems.* New York: Lothrop, Lee & Shepard Books. (Ages 6-9).

The poems in this book were written to help the author remember her days as a child in Trinidad. They include poems about the ice-cream man, the foods of the islands, the fishermen, the snails racing, the ball players, and the boogie man.

## Discussion Questions
1. Which is your favorite poem and why?
2. How do you buy ice cream from the ice-cream man?
3. What types of games do the children of these islands play?
4. What do the adults of these islands do?

## Classroom Activities

### Red Sun at Sunset
Take several photos of the sunset in your area for the children to see. Compare these with the sunsets in the picture for the poem "Red Wonder."

Provide the children with wet paper and pastels, or watercolors. Let them draw/paint pictures of sunsets from the photos that you have or develop them from memory after seeing the pictures.

If they choose, they may use these pictures as backgrounds for pictures by adding scenes from other poems from this book–boats, people, schools, or ice-cream man.

### Pull! and Tug and Pull Some More
The pattern in the poem "Pullin' Seine" presents a verb or exclamatory remark first, followed by a simple sentence telling about the verb or word(s). Children can follow this pattern and write their own poems.

### To Market
Mom carries the figs to market in her basket on her head. It's not easy to carry things on your head if you are not used to it.

Children can try this with simple non-breakable, flat, and slightly rough items. The chalkboard erasers will fit the bill, first walking, then walking the taped line on the floor and finally short relays, placing the erasers in small baskets and taking the erasers to market.

# European American

Longfellow, H.W. (1800's/1990). *Paul Revere's Ride*. New York: Dutton Children's Books. (Ages 6-9).

The poem of Longfellow is beautifully illustrated for young children.

## Discussion Questions

1. How did Paul Revere warn people about the British?
2. When did this ride take place?
3. What would they have done if the British had made their move during the day instead of at night?
4. If you want to tell people about things, how do you go about it?

# Classroom Activities

## Talking by Light

Paul Revere needs a signal to tell him how the British are going to attack. He uses a light. There are several other ways to signal people. Place the children in groups and let them generate ways that it can be done.

Give each group an assignment. One group is assigned lights; one group is assigned bells; one group is assigned phones; one group is assigned sirens; one group is assigned voices.

Each group is given a piece of paper, and they are to draw/write various ways these signals can be recognized. Example: Lights–on fire trucks, exit signs, traffic lights.

## Where Did Paul Revere Ride?

Have the children locate the original thirteen colonies on a map of the United States. Locate Boston Harbor and the Charles River. Show how Paul had to ride to another place to tell what was happening.

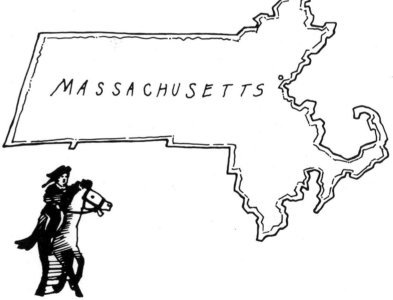

Get a large Massachusetts map for use in your classroom. Give each child a horse sticker or cutout. Have him trace the ride of Paul Revere with his horse on the map.

## What Is Silver?

Paul Revere was a silversmith. Examine things made of silver. Cut shapes out of tinfoil to make some of the silver things that Paul might have made.

# Native American

Sneve, V.D.H. (1989). *Dancing Teepees: Poems of American Indian Youth*. New York: Holiday House. (Ages 6-9).

*Dancing Teepees* is a collection of poems written by American Indian youth. Areas covered include clothes, mothers, families, homes, corn, grandparents, Mother Earth, weather.

## Discussion Questions

Which was your favorite poem? Why?

For any one poem:
1. What is this poem about?
2. How does this writer feel?
3. Has something like this happened to you before?

## Classroom Activities

### "Dancing Teepees"

The artist presents many teepees for the poem "Dancing Teepees." Let the children listen to the poem, look at the illustrations, talk about the poem and tell verbally about the teepees in the pictures.

Give each child a piece of construction paper and have him make a teepee. He may use markers, paints, crayons, construction paper and glue.

Place them all on a bulletin board entitled "Dancing Teepees."

### Native American Designs

Many of the pages show various designs of Native Americans. The parts of the designs are usually triangles, rectangles, circles, straight lines.

Have children analyze the design's form and list its colors. After several have done this, provide them with paper and crayons and let them make designs of their own.

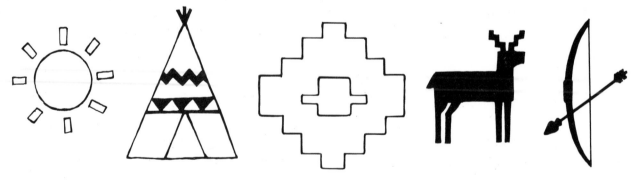

### A Poetry Book

Have the children write poems on topics of interest. Edit the poems. Type final copies. Have the children illustrate their poems and make them into a poetry book.

GA1431

# Bibliography
## Children's Books
### (Ages 4-9)

Aardema, V. (1975). *Why Mosquitoes Buzz in People's Ears*. New York: Dial. (Caldecott Medal).

Adler, D.A. (1990). *A Picture Book of Benjamin Franklin*. New York: Holiday House.

Adler, D.A. (1989). *A Picture Book of Martin Luther King, Jr.* New York: Holiday House.

Agard, J. (1989). *The Calypso Alphabet*. New York: Henry Holt and Company.

Alexander, B., and Alexander, C. (1985). *An Eskimo Family*. Minneapolis: Lerner Publications Company.

Alexander, S. (1983). *Nadia the Willful*. New York: Pantheon Books.

Appiah, S. (1988). *Amoko and Efua Bear*. New York: Macmillan Publishing Company.

Ayer, J. (1962). *The Paper-Flower Tree*. New York: Harcourt, Brace & World, Inc.

Bains, R. (1990). *Gandhi: Peaceful Warrior*. Mahwah, N.J.: Troll Associates.

Bains, R. *Harriet Tubman: The Road to Freedom*. U.S.A.: Troll Associates.

Balet, J. (1969). *The Fence*. New York: A Seymour Lawrence Delacorte Press.

Balet, J. (1965). *Joanjo*. New York: A Seymour Lawrence Delacorte Press.

Bang, M. (1983). *Dawn*. New York: William Morrow & Company.

Bannon, L. (1961). *The Gift of Hawaii*. Chicago: Albert Whitman & Company.

Bannon, L. (1939). *Manuela's Birthday*. Chicago: Albert Whitman & Company.

Behrens, J. (1989). *George Bush: Forty-First President of the United States*. Chicago: Children's Press.

Behrens, J. (1988). *Juliette Low: Founder of the Girl Scouts of America*. Chicago: Children's Press.

Behrens, J. (1965). *Soo Ling Finds a Way*. San Carlos, CA: Golden Gate Junior Books.

Belpre, P. (1969). *Santiago*. New York: Frederick Warne and Company, Inc.

Berson, H. (1982). *Barrels to the Moon*. New York: Coward, McCann & Geoghegan, Inc.

Biro, V. (1972). *The Honest Thief*. New York: Holiday House.

Black, A.D. (1973). *A Woman of the Wood: A Tale from Old Russia*. New York: Holt, Rinehart and Winston.

Blood, C.L., and Link, M. (1976, 1990). *The Goat in the Rug by Geraldine*. New York: Aladdin Books, Macmillan Publishing Company.

Bonnici, P. (1985). *The Festival*. Minneapolis: Carolrhoda Books, Inc.

Brown, M. (1982). *Shadow*. New York: Aladdin Books, Macmillan Publishing Company.

Brown, M. (1947). *Stone Soup*. New York: Charles Scribner's Sons.

Brown, T. (1986). *Hello, Amigos!* New York: Henry Holt and Company.

GA1431

Brown, T. (1991). *Lee Ann: The Story of a Vietnamese-American*. New York: G.P. Putnam's Sons.

Chief Seattle (Susan Jeffers). (1991). *Brother Eagle, Sister Sky: A Message from Chief Seattle*. New York: Dial Books.

Clark, A.N. (1979). *In the Land of Small Dragon*. New York: Viking Press.

Cohen, C.L. (1988). *The Mud Pony*. New York: Scholastic, Inc.

Cohlene, T. (1990). *Dancing Drum: A Cherokee Legend*. Mahwah, NJ: Watermill Press.

Cooper, S. (1983). *The Silver Cow: A Welsh Tale*. New York: Atheneum.

Demi. (1990). *The Empty Pot*. New York: Henry Holt and Company.

De Paola, T. (1983). *The Legend of the Bluebonnet*. New York: G.P. Putnam's Sons.

De Paola, T. (1988). *The Legend of the Indian Paintbrush*. New York: G.P. Putnam's Sons.

De Regniers, B.S. (1976). *Little Sister and the Month Brothers*. New York: Seabury Press.

Dooley, N. (1991). *Everybody Cooks Rice*. Minneapolis: Carolrhoda Books, Inc.

Dorbin, A. (1973). *Josephine's 'magination: A Tale of Haiti*. New York: Scholastic, Inc.

Duarte, M. (1968). *The Legend of the Palm Tree*. New York: Grosset & Dunlap Publishers.

Ets, M.H. (1963). *Gilberto and the Wind*. New York: Viking Press.

Feelings, M. (1974). *Jambo Means Hello: Swahili Alphabet Book*. New York: Dial.

Feeney, S. (1985). *Hawaii Is a Rainbow*. Honolulu: University of Hawaii Press.

Fisher, L.E. (1986). *The Great Wall of China*. New York: Macmillan Publishing Company.

Flack, M., and Wiese, K. (1933, 1961). *The Story About Ping*. New York: Viking Press.

Fleischman, P. (1988). *Joyful Noise*. New York: Harper & Row Publishers.

Fleisher, J. (1979). *Sitting Bull: Warrior of the Sioux*. Mahwah, N.J.: Troll Associates.

Franchere, R. (1970). *Cesar Chavez*. New York: Harper & Row Publishers.

Friedman, I.R. (1984). *How My Parents Learned to Eat*. Boston: Houghton Mifflin Company.

Friskey, M. (1959). *Indian Two Feet and His Horse*. New York: Scholastic Book Services.

Fufuka, K. (1975). *My Daddy Is a Cool Dude*. New York: The Dial Press.

Ginsburg, M. (1974). *Mushroom in the Rain*. New York: Macmillan Publishing Company.

Glasgow, A. (1971). *The Pair of Shoes*. New York: The Dial Press.

Goble, P. (1980). *The Gift of the Sacred Dog*. New York: Bradbury Press.

GA1431

Goble, P. (1985). *The Great Race of the Birds and Animals*. New York: Bradbury Press.

Goble, P. (1990). *Iktomi and the Ducks*. New York: Bradbury Press.

Gramatky, H. (1961). *Bolivar*. New York: G.P. Putnam's Sons.

Gray, N. (1988). *A Country Far Away*. New York: Orchard Books.

Greene, C. (1983). *Mother Teresa: Friend of the Friendless*. Chicago: Children's Press.

Greene, C. (1988). *Pocahontas: Daughter of a Chief*. Chicago: Children's Press.

Greenfield, E. (1976). *First Pink Light*. New York: Scholastic Book Services.

Grifalconi, A. (1986). *The Village of Round and Square Houses*. Boston: Little, Brown and Company.

Haskins, J. (1989). *Count Your Way Through Africa*. Minneapolis: Carolrhoda Books, Inc.

Haskins, J. (1989). *Count Your Way Through Mexico*. Minneapolis: Carolrhoda Books, Inc.

Havill, J. (1989). *Jamaica Tag-Along*. Boston: Houghton Mifflin Company.

Howard, Chats E.F. (1991). *Aunt Flossie's Hat (and Crab Cakes Later)*. New York: Houghton Mifflin Company.

Hoyt, H.P. (1974). *The Princess Kaiulani*. Honolulu: Island Heritage Books.

Hoyt-Goldsmith, D. (1991). *Pueblo Storyteller*. New York: Holiday House.

Hughes, M. (1967). *Why Carlo Wore a Bonnet*. New York: Lothrop, Lee & Shepard Co., Inc.

Isadora, R. (1983). *City Seen from A to Z*. New York: Greenwillow Books.

Isami, I. (1989). *The Fox's Egg*. Minneapolis: Carolrhoda Books, Inc.

Jacobsen, K. (1982). *Mexico (A New True Book)*. Chicago: Children's Press.

Joseph, L. (1990). *Coconut Kind of Day: Island Poems*. New York: Lothrop, Lee & Shepard Books.

Keats, E.J. (1969). *Goggles*. New York: Young Readers Press, Inc.

Kimmel, E.A. (1991). *The Greatest of All: A Japanese Folktale*. New York: Holiday House.

Krensky, Stephen. (1991). *Children of the Earth and Sky*. New York: Scholastic, Inc.

Kruss, J. (1970). *The Tailor and the Giant*. New York: Platt & Munk Publishers.

Lattimore, D.N. (1991). *The Flame of Peace: A Tale of the Aztecs*. Harper Trophy.

Lee, J.M. (1991). *Silent Lotus*. New York: Farrah, Straus, & Giroux.

Lessac, F. (1987). *My Little Island*. New York: Harper Trophy.

Levinson, R. (1988). *Our Home Is the Sea*. New York: E.P. Dutton.

Lewin, H. (1983). *Jafta*. Minneapolis: Carolrhoda Books, Inc.

Longfellow, H.W. (1800's/1990) *Paul Revere's Ride*. New York: Dutton Children's Books.

Louie, A. (1982). *Yeh-Shen: A Cinderella Story from China*. New York: Philomel Books.

Luenn, N. (1990). *Nessa's Fish.* New York: Atheneum.

Martel, C. (1976). *Yagua Days.* New York: The Dial Press.

Martin, Jr., B., and Archambault, J. (1966, 1987). *Knots on a Counting Rope.* New York: Henry Holt and Company.

Martin, P.M. (1968). *Kumi and the Pearl.* New York: G.P. Putnam's Sons.

McDermott, G. (1972). *Anansi the Spider: A Tale from the Ashanti.* New York: Holt, Rinehart and Winston.

McKissack, P.C. (1988). *Mirandy and Brother Wind.* New York: Alfred A. Knopf.

McNeer, M., and Ward, L. (1954). *Little Baptiste.* Boston: Houghton Mifflin Company.

Mendez, P. (1989). *The Black Snowman.* New York: Scholastic, Inc.

Miles, M. (1971). *Annie and the Old One.* Boston: Little, Brown and Company.

Musgrove, M. (1976). *Ashanti to Zulu: African Traditions.* New York: Dial Books. (Caldecott Medal).

National Geographic Society. (October, 1991). *National Geographic,* "1491: America Before Columbus." Washington, D.C.

Ortiz, S. (1977, 1988). *The People Shall Continue.* San Francisco, CA: Children's Book Press.

Osinski, A. (1987). *The Navajo.* Chicago: Children's Press.

Politi, L. (1964). *Lito and the Clown.* New York: Charles Scribner's Sons.

Politi, L. (1960). *Moy Moy.* New York: Charles Scribner's Sons.

Politi, L. (1975). *Mr. Fong's Toy Shop.* New York: Charles Schibner's Sons.

Politi, L. (1963). *Rosa.* New York: Charles Scribner's Sons. (toys, school)

Quigley, L. (1959). *The Blind Men and the Elephant.* New York: Charles Scribner's Sons.

Rosenthal, B. (1986). *Lynette Woodard, the First Female Globetrotter.* Chicago: Children's Press.

Rylant, C. (1982). *When I Was Young in the Mountains.* New York: E.P. Dutton.

Say, A. (1990). *El Chino.* Boston: Houghton Mifflin Company.

Say, A. (1991). *Tree of Cranes.* Boston: Houghton Mifflin Company.

Simon, N. (1967). *What Do I Say?* Chicago: Albert Whitman & Company.

Sneve, V.D.H. (1989). *Dancing Teepees: Poems of American Indian Youth.* New York: Holiday House.

Stanek, M. (1989). *I Speak English for My Mom.* Niles, IL: Albert Whitman & Company.

Steptoe, J. (1987). *Mufaro's Beautiful Daughters.* New York: Lothrop, Lee & Shepard Books.

Surat, M.M. (1983). *Angel Child, Dragon Child.* New York: Scholastic, Inc.

Tejima. (1990). *Ho-Limlim: A Rabbit Tale from Japan.* New York: Philomel Books.

Todd, B. (1972). *Juan Patricio.* New York: G.P. Putnam's Sons.

Turner, Ann. (1985). *Dakota Dugout.* New York: Macmillan Publishing Company.

GA1431

Udry, J.M. (1966). *What Mary Jo Shared*. Chicago: Albert Whitman & Company.

Varga, J. (1969). *Janko's Wish*. New York: William Morrow & Company.

Verheyden-Hilliard, M.E. (1985). *Engineer from the Comanche Nation: Nancy Wallace*. Bethesda, MD: The Equity Institute.

Waters, K., and Slovenz-Low, M. (1990). *Lion Dancer: Ernie Wan's Chinese New Year*. New York: Scholastic, Inc.

White Deer of Autumn. (1983, 1991). *Ceremony in the Circle of Life*. Hillsboro, OR: Beyond Words Publishing, Inc.

Williams, K.L. (1991). *When Africa Was Home*. New York: Orchard Books.

Xiong, Blia, and Spagnoli, C. (1989). *Nine-in-One, Grr! Grr!* San Francisco, CA: Children's Book Press.

Yashima, M., and Yashima, T. (1954). *Plenty to Watch*. New York: Viking Press.

Yashima, T. (1955). *Crow Boy*. New York: Viking Press. (A Caldecott Honor Book).

Yashima, T. (1958). *Umbrella*. New York: Viking Press.

Yolen, J., and Moser, B. (1990). *Sky Dogs*. San Diego: Harcourt Brace Jovanovich Publishers.

Young, E. (1989). *Lon Po Po: A Red-Riding Hood Story from China*. New York: Scholastic, Inc. (Caldecott Medal).

GA1431

# Series of Books

*Crowell Biographies*. New York. Thomas Y. Crowell, Company.

*Easy Menu Ethnic Cookbooks*. Minneapolis: Lerner Publishing Company.
A series of twenty plus different books with simple menus from Africa, the Caribbean, China, England, France, Germany, Greece, Hungary, India, Israel, Italy, Japan, Korea, Lebanon, Mexico, Norway, Poland, Russia, Spain, Thailand and Vietnam.

*Ethnic and Traditional Holidays*. Chicago: Children's Press.
A series of six books showing photographs of holiday celebrations for Mexicans, Chinese, Jews, Native Americans and Samoans.

*Famous Friends Series*. Carthage, IL: Good Apple, Inc.
Famous Friends is a series of six teacher idea books with seven children's stories imbedded in each. The individual books are *Founders, Pathfinders, Presidential Leaders, Inventors, Outstanding Women* and *Legendary Heroes*. Children's stories are followed by vocabulary words, discussion questions and activities.

*Great African Americans Series*. Enslow Publishers, Inc. Hillside, NJ.

Haskins, J. (1989). *Count Your Way Through Africa*. Minneapolis: Carolrhoda Books, Inc.
A series of counting books that tell something about the country for each number presented. Africa and Mexico are two of the books.

*Indian Two Feet Books*. Chicago: Children's Press.
A series of six books about Indian Two Feet written between 1959 and 1980. The books included are about the alphabet, his eagle feather, his horse, riding alone, a wolf cub and a grizzly bear.

Lee, M. (1989). *The Seminoles*. New York: Franklin Watts.
(Others in the series include *The Apaches and Navajos, The Iroquois, The Shoshoni, The Sioux* and *The Totem Pole Indians of the Northwest*.)
A series of six books that give vivid descriptions and histories of the life, customs, and art of the major Native American Indian tribes.

*Picture-Story Biographies*. Chicago: Children's Press.
  A series of twenty-nine books which depict biographies of various people from around the world.  Photos and large print make the books nice for second grade through fourth grade.

*Rookie Biographies*. Chicago: Children's Press.
  A series of twenty-two biographies from around the world written specifically for k-3.

Spizzirri, L. (1981-1989). *Educational Coloring Books*. Rapid City, SD: Spizzirri Publishing, Inc.
  *California Indians, Southwest Indians, Northwest Indians, Northeast Indians, Eskimos, Plains Indians.*
  A series of coloring books that provide one page of information (tribe name, language, where they lived, kind of house, what they ate and interesting facts) and one coloring page per tribe.

*Sports Stars*. Chicago: Children's Press.
  A series of sixteen books.

*The New True Books*. Chicago: Children's Press.
  A series of twenty-seven books available on different Native American tribes.
  A series of twenty-five books available on different countries.

*Visual Geography Series*. Minneapolis: Lerner Publications Company.
  A series of  books that give a brief introduction to the history, land, people, economy and government of forty-eight countries in Africa, Middle East, Southwest Asia and the Americas. Each book contains many excellent pictures and maps.

*Young Discovery Library*. Chicago: Children's Press.
  A series of thirty-six books on various topics, some of which are about other countries and about living in other lands.

GA1431

# Teacher Resource Books and Posters

Benarde. A. (1970). *Games from Many Lands*. New York: The Lion Press.

Bierhorst, J. (1987). *Doctor Coyote: A Native American's Aesop's Fables*. New York: Macmillan.

Bredekamp, S. (Ed.). (1987). *Developmentally Appropriate Practice in Early Childhood Programs Serving Children from Birth Through Age 8: Expanded Edition*. Washington, D.C.: NAEYC.

Bryan, A. (1991). *All Night, All Day: A Child's First Book of African-American Spirituals*. New York: Atheneum.

Caduto, M.J., and Bruchac, J. (1988, 1989). *Keepers of the Earth: Native American Stories and Environmental Activities for Children*. Golden, CO: Fulcrum, Inc.

Courlander, H., and Herzog, G. (1947, 1974). *The Cow-Tail Switch and Other West African Stories*. New York: Henry Holt and Company.
> A collection of eighteen stories–no illustrations.

D'Aulaire I., and D'Aulaire, E.P. (1962). *D'Aulaires' Book of Greek Myths*. New York: Doubleday.

Delacre, L. (1990). *Las Navidades: Popular Christmas Songs from Latin America*. New York: Scholastic, Inc.

Derman-Sparks, L., and the ABC Task Force. (1989). *Anti-Bias Curriculum: Tools for Empowering Young Children*. Washington, D.C.: NAEYC.

De Van Etten, T.P. (1990). *Spanish-American Folktales*. Little Rock: August House Publishers, Inc.

Durell, A. (1989). *The Diane Goode Book of American Folk Tales and Songs*. New York: E.P. Dutton.

Kennedy, P.E. (1971). *North American Indian Design Coloring Book*. New York: Dover Publishing Inc.

Lobel, A. (1980). *Fables*. New York: Scholastic, Inc.

Mayo, G.W. (1988). *Star Tales: North American Indian Stories About the Stars*. New York: Walker.

Mayol, L.B. (1943). *The Talking Totem Pole: The Tales It Told to the Indian Children of the Northwest*. Portland, OR: Binfords & Mort Publishers.

Miles, C., and Bovis, P. (1969, 1977). *American Indian & Eskimo Basketry*. Santa Fe, NM: Pierre Bovis.

*Native Monthly Reader*. P.O. Box 217, Crestone, CO 81131.
> The *Native Monthly Reader* is designed for young adults, middle school through high school providing information about the Native American cultural background. It is published eight times a year.

Ney, M.W. (1977). *Indian America: A Geography of North American Indians*. Cherokee, NC: Cherokee Publications.

Pugh, E. (1971). *More Tales from the Welsh Hills*. New York: Dodd, Mead and Company.

Rieske, W.M. (1981). *Primitive Rock Art Glossary: Subjects and Symbols* (poster). Salt Lake City, UT: Historic Indian Publishers.
> Other posters available are *Contributions of Native Americans; Edibles; Indian Dwellings and Homes*.

Robertson, D. (Storyteller). (1971). *Fairy Tales from the Philippines*. New York: Dodd, Mead and Company.

Sakade, F. (Ed.). (1958). *Japanese Children's Favorite Stories*. Rutland, VT: Charles E. Tuttle Company.

Spizzirri, L. *Educational Coloring Books: California Indians, Southwest Indians, Northwest Indians, Northeast Indians, Eskimos, Plains Indians*.

Tatum, C. (Ed.). (1990). *Mexican American Literature*. Orlando: Harcourt Brace Jovanovich Publishers.

Wyndham, R. (Ed.). (1968). *Chinese Mother Goose Rhymes*. Cleveland: The World Publishing Company.

Yeats, W.B. (Ed.). *Irish Folk Stories and Fairy Tales*. New York: Grosset & Dunlap.

Zitkala-Sa. (1985). *Old Indian Legends*. Lincoln, NE: University of Nebraska Press.

GA1431